Embroidered Pictures

*Detail from **Eugenia's Lemon Tree** (see page 33)*

Embroidered Pictures

DOROTHY TUCKER

A&C BLACK · LONDON

First published 1994

A & C Black (Publishers) Limited
35 Bedford Row, London WC1R 4JH

ISBN 0–7136–3737–4

© 1994 A & C Black (Publishers) Limited

Stitch diagrams by Barbara Pegg
Design by Janet Watson

A CIP catalogue record for this book is available from the British Library.

Typeset in Horley Old Style by Wyvern Typesetting Ltd, Bristol.
Printed and bound in Great Britain by Butler & Tanner Ltd, Frome.

Acknowledgements

I am indebted to:

all of the embroiderers whose work I have included, for their generous response to my requests for photographs, drawings and background information; and to Surgeet Hussain and her friends for their help on Kanthas;

Anne Watts, my editor, for her encouragement and guidance;

Dudley Moss for many of the excellent photographs;

Barbara Pegg for transforming rough sketches into clear stitch diagrams;

Lynn Szygenda, the Curator at the Embroiderers' Guild, for persuading me to look and then to ask who, where, when and why before how!;

Constance Howard who continues to inspire my love for embroidery;

Terry, my husband, for all his support, and for word-processing the text;

and, last but not least, a thank you to my family and friends who waited patiently to see more of us both 'when the book is finished'.

Contents

Detail from **Feeding Chickens**
(see page 57)

The stitch as such, probably evolved very slowly . . . Gradually rhythmic movements began to develop into stitches which could be remembered . . . Stitches were handed down from generation to generation, family to family, the repertoire being added to by travellers returning from foreign countries. They were invented by accident or intent, gradually becoming an international language . . . Today embroidery is open for experiment and stitches are a means of expressing original ideas in a lively, personal way.

Constance Howard, from her preface to *The Constance Howard Book of Stitches* (Batsford, 1979)

Stitches alone are like words in a dictionary. They need a thought or a theme to make them speak.

Crissie White in *Embroidery* vol. 31 no. 1 Spring 1980

What is Embroidery . . . It is a synthesis of drawing, design, use of materials, colour and stitching . . . They form a unity within which by changing emphasis all manner of expression and experiment is possible.

Kathleen White in *Embroidery* vol. 15 no. 4 Winter 1964

Detail from **Head of Christ** (see page 78)

Preface

Embroidered Pictures began with a search for embroidered images from the world around us, objects and scenes from everyday life, narratives, symbols or dreams.

The book evolved not as the history of picture embroidery, nor as a source book for designs and technique, but as a personal notebook of first-hand studies to inspire and inform contemporary work. These studies include something of the history or the context of a chosen piece, the drawing or source of its design, its composition, the materials, and the way the simplest and most familiar embroidery stitches have been used.

Three distinct themes emerged: the people who created the embroideries, the images and messages they conveyed through their pictures, and the way in which the embroideries are composed and stitched.

The book contains three sets of illustrations concerned with composition. There are drawings and working designs prepared by Audrey Walker for a major commission, and drawings by Jean Draper. There are stitch diagrams (with notes on the materials employed) and eight stitch samples worked to explore how the embroiderers concerned used their stitches to draw, create tone and mix colour.

The work I have included by no means represents a complete range of embroidered pictures or possible story/image formats. The book simply aims to share a number of different pieces chosen for their expressive qualities and the way they have been put together. I would like to think that it will encourage you to find examples of your own to explore through looking, reading, drawing and stitching. I hope that you will share my discovery that there is as much inspiration to be found from asking who embroidered a picture, when, where and why, as from knowing how it is stitched, and that there is much to be gained from giving ourselves more time to examine an embroidery in detail.

Key to symbols:

 This symbol indicates that the stitch is worked best with the fabric stretched over a ring or frame.

 This symbol indicates that the stitch is worked best with the fabric in the hands.

NTF These initials indicate that the needle is not taken through the fabric.

A Paracas Mantle

PERU, *c.* 600 BC

This mantle was found on the arid Paracas peninsula on the southern coast of Peru in 1927 when some burial places were excavated by Julio C Telo. Mummies were found in a crouching position in baskets. They were covered in ritual garments, then wrapped in layers and layers of coarsely woven cloth. They had been preserved because the hot desert sands had kept the air out of the deep tombs where they had been placed. The élite dead were found wrapped in up to sixty woven cloths embroidered with designs which related to one another.

The Paracas mantles, as these are now known, must have involved many skilled people in the production of spun fibres, weaving and embroidery. Different types of needles were found during the excavations, and up to 190 shades of thread were recorded. The dyes were obtained from plant, animal and mineral sources. Fragments show that the embroidery was stitched into plain-weave cloth with fine thread spun from the fleece of camelids such as llamas, alpacas and vicuñas.

In reading to find out more about the piece I came across an article written by Anne Paul and Susan A Niles, the outcome of a research project in the National Museum of Anthropology and Archaeology in Lima. A team examined sixty garments from a single funeral bundle and chose to concentrate on an unfinished mantle because it revealed the way in which the embroidered design had been built up. The team's first-hand observations give a fascinating insight into the possible production of a Paracas Mantle.

A figure-by-figure examination revealed that many people were involved. The most illuminating information came from looking at the kind of errors made by less skilled workers. Many mantles involve a complex four-way pattern of alternation that reverses one or two figure details in both an up-and-down and right-and-left pattern. Sometimes a worker got the direction of the knees wrong although the stave correct, or used the wrong shaped stave, or embroidered a hand-held knife pointing downwards. Such errors suggest that they were not working from templates nor following a completed drawing. Skilled workers seem to have counted threads to space the figures and regulate their size. Large **running stitches** were used to mark out significant parts of the design field but no trace could be found of stitches used to mark out the columns.

Initially the silhouette of the images and then details such as the eyes, mouth and costume detail would have been outlined in one colour of thread. Such outlining could be corrected easily but, more significantly perhaps, it would allow the possibility of 'assembly line production'. Anne Paul suggests that the artists drawing these designs referred both to the shapes of things in the world around them and the iconic traditions of their culture in a way that was open to individual interpretation. There is evidence that the most skilled workers established the overall design and it is possible that they monitored the work of the less skilled workers. New workers may have learned to embroider by copying small, relatively simple figures between those embroidered by skilled workers.

A Paracas Mantle Peru
Paracas Culture, c. 600 BC
261cm ✕146cm
National Museum of Anthropology and Archaeology, Lima

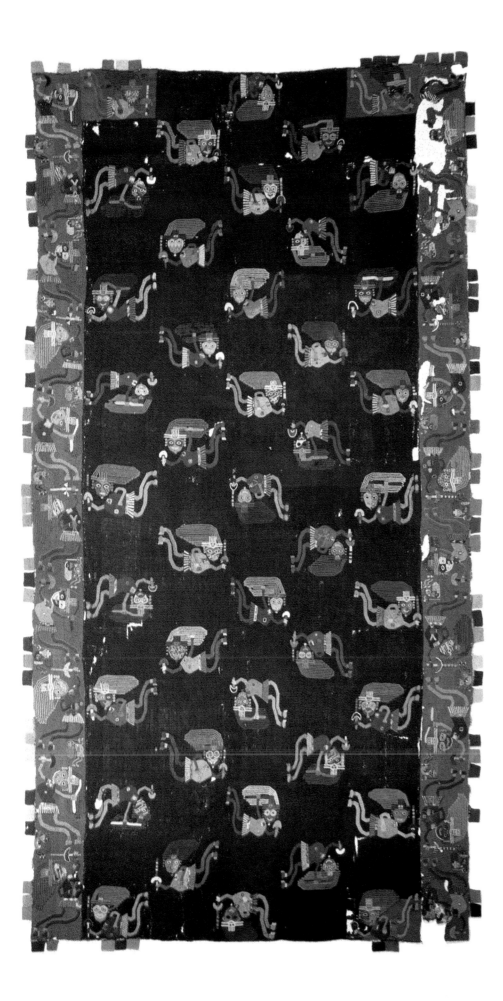

Skilled and unskilled work was consistent with the use of different threads. It is probable that the mantle was worked on simultaneously by both skilled and clumsy workers. If this was so then the cloth must have been stretched on some sort of frame to maintain the tension and keep the work in easy reach of everyone. A frame would enable workers to sit side by side or on opposite sides of the mantle. The work seems to have proceeded in columns moving towards the centre. The workers may have swapped sides to complete their column in a return journey. This would avoid the awkward task of embroidering an 'upside down' motif.

The outlines were a guide for the areas to be filled with embroidery. Little bits of thread pulled through the cloth and then snipped seem to indicate which colour was to be used. Contrasting sets of colour were favoured, such as light pink next to dark blue, sky blue next to dark gold. Light green is often found next to red, and dark green next to a light gold. The researchers had the impression that the colour had been evenly distributed across the piece. It was as if the balance of colour may have been masterminded by a colour expert. The background to the images was filled in first with neat parallel rows of stitching. Then the arms, legs, faces, costume elements, headdresses and hand-held items were embroidered. **Stem stitch** was employed throughout. Working the background and then the images as two separate operations produced a design which is still visually clear and legible.

What emerges is a design built up through a process of working together collectively and a format which, although set by 'experts', has room for differences in individual skills. To Anne Paul and Susan A Niles, the very fact that errors remained uncorrected and the incomplete mantle was included in the bundle suggests that contributing to the piece was perhaps as important as the production of something perfect. For us this mantle could provide a useful model for group work in which an artist masterminds the essential elements of a design but the embroidery is as elementary as filling outlined shapes with colour. The checkered board containing different variations of a set design offers a simple format. The idea of including pictures in such a way that they can be read diagonally as well as up and down is full of potential for textile design.

Photo detail 1

The colour, layout and design elements of the mantle are both subtle and complex. The figures are arranged in horizontal and vertical rows in a distinctly organised way. The placing of the figures and the direction of the details clearly relate to the weave of the fabric. The hair strands out following the grain horizontally whilst the toes lock into the weave vertically. Arms, staves and knives reinforce this sense of an underlying grid. The mantle is an example of a colour block design, i.e. the images consist of curved and rectilinear shapes, each stitched entirely in one colour to create solid areas of colour. Each figure faces the viewer and stares out with large open eyes. The heads are large in relation to the tunic-clad bodies. Both knees always point in the same direction but sometimes they are set to be the same as those of an adjacent figure and sometimes opposite. There are differences in gesture and detail. There is no right way up. Many figures are upside down and give an impression of flying or floating. The whole piece is strikingly beautiful and strange.

Photo detail 2

The stitching is limited to **stem stitch** throughout the embroidered mantle. Worked in close vertical rows, one row up and one row down with the slant in the opposite direction, this gives a knitted appearance. Worked in horizontal rows it looks woven.

(a) A single line of **stem stitch** used to outline an image.

(b) Rows of **stem stitch** worked to give a woven appearance and used to fill in background colour.

(c) Rows of **stem stitch** worked to give a knitted appearance and used to fill the outlined shapes with colour.

7cm

7cm

Part of an embroidered shawl from Paracas   Peru
Early Mazca culture, AD 100–600 (T 69–1933)
16cm × 46cm
Victoria & Albert Museum, London
*Embroidery worked with wools on woollen ground, **stem stitch** employed throughout.*

Water-soluble coloured pencils were used for the second drawing. These are ideal for making colour studies in museums. Later a light brush with water will sharpen the colour. A collection of coloured papers or yarn samples can provide a way of recording colours accurately for future reference without risking any damage to the textiles being studied.

These drawings were made from a fragment of an embroidered shawl from Peru found in the Textile Collection at the Victoria & Albert Museum, London.

The fragment is mounted in a glass frame which can be withdrawn from its case and taken to a table to study. Having previously seen only illustrations of Peruvian textiles I was totally unprepared for the size and delicacy of the work. The whole fragment only measures 46cm × 16cm. Each block is only 7cm square. At first it is difficult to distinguish the stitches from the material they are worked on.

The figures are contained within a checkerboard of solid dark green squares on a red woollen ground. Worked in close vertical rows of stem stitch these have a woven appearance. The thread employed is a very fine smooth wool, dyed dark green, red or yellow, purple/brown or dark blue. In places, dark green outlines round some figure shapes can be seen. The rows of stitches which fill the shapes with colour follow the outlines instead of the vertical stitch direction of the green ground.

When I stitched a sample to scale with the original it was soon evident that the finest wool available to me was no match to the thread spun by the Peruvians (see photo on previous page).

As I drew, I discovered feline things: side whiskers and pointed chins. I felt rather than saw the sinuous bodies of cats. Then, an even more subtle note, I found that lines of stitches between the eyes perfectly suggest a cat's nose. But the open eyes and smiling mouths, the nipples and navels, and phallic appendages add up to neither man nor beast. As I drew, it became easier as I recognised the grid common to all the figure blocks. Without much more practice I could draw a block from memory!

I later read that the Paracas people thought of the world in terms of the live forces within it: Earth, Fire, Air and Water. Plants and animals were drawn both literally as they are seen in the physical world, and metaphorically.

Rows of images like these function somewhere between writing and pictures, which can be decoded to give social, religious and environmental information. In this way each mantle is invested with symbolic meanings that were of great importance to their makers.

Anne Paul suggests that the pampas cats which inhabited the crops the Paracas farmers cultivated may have been so strongly associated with the land that they became a visual metaphor for the life-giving properties of the earth. And so embroidered cats may be connected to earth cults in which feline costumes and masks are worn by ritual dancers.

It's Alright
PRIMMY CHORLEY

It's Alright *Primmy Chorley 1991*
approx. 36cm × 50cm
Private collection (photo: Peter Chorley)

Primmy includes herself in this picture. We see her pushing a baby in a pram with a small figure in tow, accompanied by the family pets. To me, *It's Alright* is part of an inner journey in which turbulent emotional feelings are expressed by the threatening movement and form of the tree. This would dominate the composition but for the angels which fill the spaces between its branches. If read from left to right, as the tree indicates, the embroidery seems to be about Primmy's moving towards hope and life, which are symbolised by the rainbow above her and the sun ahead of her.

Angels are divine messengers or ministering spirits in picture form: a concept perhaps not so dissimilar from the figures found on the Paracas Mantle? After all, angels are depicted as humans – with wings to indicate that they are representatives from the spiritual world. When one comes to think about it, angels are not the only symbolic picture images still in common currency today.

It's Alright was one of eight pieces shown by Primmy Chorley at the Embroiderers' Guild in an exhibition selected by Audrey Walker and called 'In Context' in December 1990. The pieces are about Primmy's life: *Love and Happiness, A Marriage, Despair, Birth, For you Jessie, The Goodbye,* are pictures about events before the family moved to North Wales. *It's Alright* expresses an experience which gave Primmy a sense of total serenity and the realisation that, whatever happens, life goes on.

The cottage in Wales was at one time used by slate miners who slept there on weekdays. It is a fairly isolated place. The weather can be extreme and the wilderness around seems to reclaim the garden as soon as it can. Primmy educates her children at home. After she left art school, any creative work that she did was for the family. She decorated the children's clothes and made them dolls but now much of her time is spent on just keeping the place in good repair.

She was only able to complete the pieces for the exhibition by giving herself an hour each day to sew. Because she has so little time she works straight onto the cloth. This means that there is always an element of surprise which she enjoys and, of course, the children often add their ideas as she sews. Her daughter is beginning to stitch pictures of her own.

Over the years Primmy has built up a notebook of words, ideas and colours with the odd drawing or two. This has become a diary for her. Now she wants to get all these 'memories sewn up as pictures'.

She says that although she has made her pictures to last, what matters most is that they express her feelings. Technique is very low on her list of priorities. She does not like decorative stitchery and uses only basic stitches such as **stem**, **running** and **buttonhole**. She uses bits and pieces of fabric recycled from the family's old clothing; some scraps are 'precious bits' with memories attached.

Primmy likes to think of her work as being passed on amongst her family to record memories they have shared, as old quilts do, rather than as 'art'.

*(a) Notice how **running stitch** worked mainly in cream coloured wools saves the white angels from visually disappearing and adds to the sense of movement. It is a stitch closely associated with quilted textiles.*

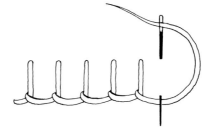

*(b) The figures are created from simple cut-out shapes of fabric with cotton embroidery threads applied as **buttonhole stitch**.*

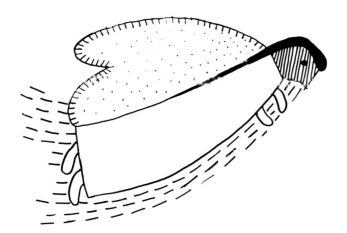

*(c) It is interesting to compare Primmy Chorley's use of **stem stitch** to draw her tree with the way the Paracas embroiderers use it first to outline shapes and then to fill or surround them with colour. The trees, rainbow and sun are embroidered in wools.*

The Bayeux Tapestry

FRANCE, ELEVENTH CENTURY

Illustrations of the Bayeux Tapestry take me back to childhood and time spent drawing arms and armour, modes of transport and battle in Norman times! But when I saw the Tapestry first hand at the Museum in Bayeux, all these associations fell away because the story is communicated so directly. The clear gestures and expressions, and the intimate scale and vitality of the embroidery quickly engage lines of very absorbed people along its length. It is approximately seventy metres long and half a metre wide. Essentially it is a drama in visual form simple enough for a child to read but of equal interest to adults. Despite signs in the Museum that request silence, people cannot help but point and share their appreciation of the story with each other.

It would be interesting to compare the original response of the people who first saw the tapestry with that of the tourists today. People in the eleventh century were for the most part illiterate but were used to reading Biblical stories presented in picture form. An inventory of Bayeux Cathedral's Treasury in 1476 states that the Tapestry was hung during a festival of relics. Until the eighteenth century it was displayed once a year in July in the nave of the cathedral. The rest of the year it was rolled up and kept in a chest. Today's viewers are furnished by the Museum with tape recorded loops of thoroughly-researched and carefully-presented background information.

Historians generally agree that the Tapestry was commissioned by Odo, Bishop of Bayeux, who was William the Conqueror's half brother and who was made Earl of Kent, an area famous for its embroidery. It was probably made between 1066 and 1077. Historically, it is the primary source of our knowledge of the Norman Conquest. Technically, it is a rare example of its kind from the early Middle Ages.

Some scholars think it was made in Normandy, others in England. Embroidered hangings were common in the homes of Anglo-Saxon aristocracy. Where the work of designing it was carried out will probably never be known but there was an important school of drawing at Canterbury which produced illuminated manuscripts. The formation of the embroidered letters has many typically English elements. Studies of the drawing of both faces and figures also suggest similarities with English manuscripts, e.g. the heads in the Tapestry have similar round features and big jaws. The scenes may have been drawn by a draughtsman before they were embroidered. The quality of line is, however, considerably modified when stitched.

The Tapestry consists of eight pieces of coarse linen sewn together end to end. Despite being called a tapestry it is in fact all hand embroidered. The stitching has been carried out in fine, naturally-dyed wools in a limited range of colours: terracotta and old gold, olive green and blue, dark blue black. The colour is not used naturalistically. A horse may be blue, and no attempt is made to represent flesh tones. Faces and hands are simply expressed in outline. These contrasts between light and dark, unstitched spaces of linen ground or solid masses of embroidery, the movement of the horses and the gestures of the figures, all add to the intensely lively and ongoing quality of the narrative.

A unified and simple beauty is created by a balance between open outlines and closely-packed areas of colour on the plain bleached linen. It is interesting that in the eighteenth century the tapestry was thought to be unfinished, not completely filled in.

The Bayeux Tapestry   *11th century*
This embroidery is thought to have been commissioned by Odo, Bishop of Bayeux, and made between 1066 and 1077.
approx. 50cm × 70m
Musée de la Tapisserie de Bayeux (photos by special permission of the Ville de Bayeux)

Astrologers announce an evil omen for Harold.

Norman spies inform William of the events following Edward's death.

The embroiderers stitched the Tapestry in **laid and couched work** with outlines of **stem stitch**.

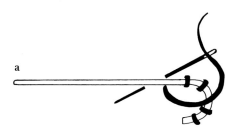

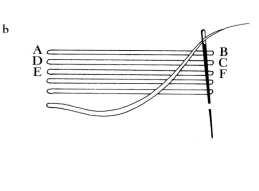

(a) **Couching**: from the French 'coucher' which means 'to lay down'. It was used a great deal by Medieval embroiderers as an effective and economical way of outlining or covering large areas. The stitches lie on the surface of the material and are anchored by very small stitches taken through to the back of the work. This was important when threads were scarce or costly to produce. The direction of laid and couched threads was used to produce certain calculated effects.

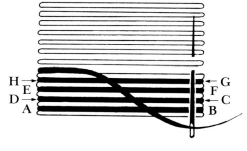

(b) **Bayeux stitch** is worked with the material stretched on a frame. The laid threads are stitched in two journeys. Starting from the widest part of the shape, the first set of stitches across leave free exactly the width of a thread, the spaces between are then filled by a second set of stitches on a return journey. The threads are so close together that no material shows between them. When the shape is covered, the laid threads are anchored down perpendicularly with a couching thread of a contrasting colour or weight. The couching threads are placed and stitched down about 0·5cm apart. The filled shapes are then outlined with stem stitch.

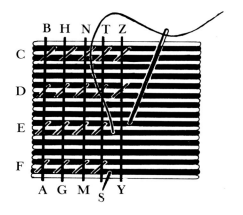

William orders an invasion fleet to be built.

The fleet is being built.

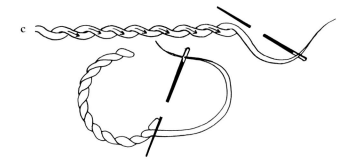

(c) **Stem stitch** is mainly used to outline shapes, but worked in circles it depicts chain-mail suits of armour.

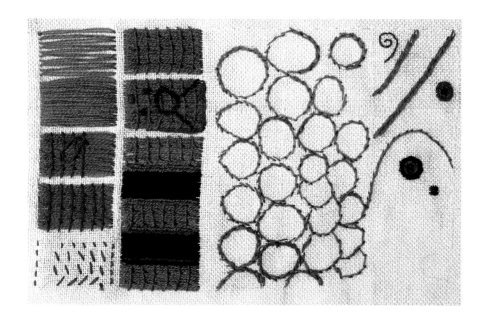

Notice how the clarity and liveliness of the embroidery depend as much on strong contrasts in the density of the stitching as on colour. This stitched sample, not worked to the scale of the original, illustrates how the stitching provides outlines or shapes filled with colour. Within these an infinite number of variations are possible.

The first blocks are stitched in different colours to demonstrate the sequence of work. The wrong side of the embroidery shows an economical use of thread. Notice how inevitable irregularities in the stitching are lost when a block is couched in the same colour.

Once I had settled into a rhythm I found I could complete a square inch of bayeux stitch within ten minutes! This gives some insight into the time it must have taken to complete the whole tapestry.

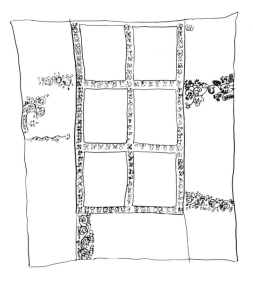

Half the Guicciardini Quilt depicting the Tristan legend (Victoria & Albert Museum)

There are many other examples of narrative embroidered textiles. Sometimes the scenes are contained within a design divided into shaped compartments. More often than not, scenes are arranged in blocks, usually with borders. When we want to tell a story through pictures or record a sequence of historical events, it is difficult to know how to sort out our ideas into a viable design. A comparison of different narrative pieces from the past and from other cultures could provide a basic pattern to follow and some solutions to some very tricky problems. For example, how can the progress of time be indicated? Or, how can quite disparate elements be combined?

The tapestry exploits only a limited range of colour and stitch. Notice how the scale of the buildings, figures and horses varies. The Tapestry is remarkable because the scenes are not boxed into a rigid format. Where necessary, buildings or ships encroach upon the border above and bodies fall into the borders below the battle scenes. The story moves forward without our being aware of the subtle visual signals which lead us on. Various devices, also found in illuminated medieval manuscripts are used to introduce breaks or continuity between scenes. For example, the beginning or end of an episode is frequently marked by a tree or tower. These can be thought of as punctuation marks in picture form. When the story line has been followed and enjoyed, it is worth going back to the beginning to appreciate these design features in more detail.

Detail of the Syon Cope which illustrates 14 scenes from the life of Christ in lozenges like these

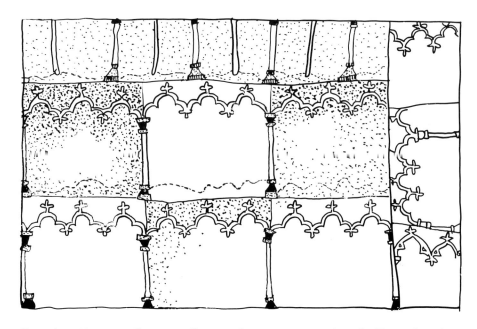

Part of a 14th century German wallhanging depicting 22 scenes from the Tristan legend (Victoria & Albert Museum)

The Skater
NORMA ANDERSON

The Skater   *Norma Anderson*   *1991*
31cm × 38cm
Private collection (photo: Dudley Moss)

After stitching a near to exact copy of a figure on horseback from the Bayeux Tapestry as part of an historical study, Norma Anderson embroidered this contemporary image. Although she exploits **bayeux** *and* **stem stitch** *and uses wools on linen, her work is not a pastiche. Her approach to colour and tone is significantly different in the way that she has used closely-graded tones of green and red to express movement and speed. Along with this complete panel are her preliminary colour studies and drawings, stitched sample and her final design.*

One Thousand Years of Monarchy

AUDREY WALKER

Edgar, the first King of England, was crowned in the Abbey at Bath in AD 973. In 1973 the City of Bath wanted to commemorate a thousand years of Monarchy. As part of the civic celebrations it commissioned Audrey Walker to design and embroider a panel to hang in the Pump Room. The commission required that it should record a thousand years of Monarchy, that the colours should be complementary to the panel's setting, and that gold should be included.

Audrey Walker trained as a painter at the Edinburgh College of Art and the Slade School of Fine Art in London. When she became interested in embroidery she attended some part-time classes with Margaret Nicholson, and subsequently became a member of the Embroiderers' Guild and the '62 Group.

As the inspiration for her paintings and embroidery springs mainly from an interest in landscape, the commission was a challenge not only in scale but also in subject matter. It presented her with new problems to solve, not least how to contain a thousand years of history in a single panel. After all, it had taken more than sixty pictures and over seventy metres of cloth for the Bayeux Tapestry to illustrate what had happened in 1066!

The Pump Room is elegant and spacious. Its windows look out on the warm stone walls and green waters of the Roman Baths. In 1973 it was decorated in pale turquoise and white. From these surroundings Audrey Walker selected turquoises, blues, greens, greys and creams as the predominant colours for the panel which she was to work.

Before she could begin to design the panel she had to do a great deal of historical research. As she read, the violence of the continuous political struggles which had taken place between the Royal Houses and against potential invaders began to form a moving pattern of men and horses, flags and armies in her mind's eye. Her research took her to the British Museum and to look at the tombs in Westminster Abbey (*preparatory drawing 1*).

Only when she saw the connection between embroidery and the Monarchy through banners and flags did the structure for the design fall into place. The idea of nine vertical strips to represent the nine Royal Houses provided her with the means of containing the time span and all fifty monarchs. She decided to place a familiar portrait of a monarch at the top of each strip to represent a named Royal House, and then at the foot of the strips, to list all the other monarchs accordingly (*preparatory drawing 2*).

These nine portraits were carefully adapted and worked separately in a range of gold threads and gold kid applied to fine muslin, and added to the panel later. Notice how the thin Kings are given wide thrones to fill the width of the strip (*photo details*). The number of monarchs in each Royal House varies. Fitting lettering as different in length as Mary and Elizabeth into the strips presented a problem. This was solved by moving letters cut out in different sizes up and down within the strips until they settled comfortably.

When I went to see the panel the Pump Room was crowded with visitors. More often than not it was the recognition of Henry VIII or the image of the present Queen which seemed to make people take a second look. This familiarity with a portrait seemed to provide a lead into looking at the embroidery with more interest.

The nine-strip solution to the structure of the design left the centre of the panel free to include the image of the moving armies. Audrey Walker wanted to use this to express the violence and struggle for power which had taken place. For this section she looked at authentic drawings and paintings of major battles and extracted some key details (*preparatory drawing 1*). She then drew these together into a continuous flow of images, which begins with the Vikings and ends with the bombing of St Paul's Cathedral in the Second World War. As she says, 'Chain mail and horses to khaki and cannon'. Her preparatory drawings at this stage gave an overall impression open to further interpretation in fabric and thread (*preparatory drawing 3*).

The first of a series of working drawings and designs presented by Audrey Walker for **One Thousand Years of Monarchy**: *research drawings through which some key details were extracted from contemporary drawings and paintings of major battles.*

figures + surrounding areas treated together in simplified areas of gold kid + textured areas of gold threads etc + very controlled areas of colour introduced

WINDSOR

SAXON

STUART

TUDOR

or

TUDOR

TOP OF PANEL.

start from "familiar" portrait so that the image can be formalised by translation into fabrics yet remain "recognisable". Figures, lettering + surrounding area to be seen as a whole.

The second of a series of working drawings and designs presented by Audrey Walker for **One Thousand Years of Monarchy**: *some research drawings for the nine Royal portraits.*

decorative top
panel of monarchs

gold work –
padded.
gold threads
freely textured
patchwork of
rich silks too.

Central area –
figures – patches of fabrics.
linear outlines suggesting
details of heads, armour,
swords, arrows, rifles.
linking areas to give a feeling
of continual movement in
free texture of stitches
– (straight stitches,
cretan, herringbone,
open chain,
knots, seeding etc)

COLOURS white & cream
muted, gauzy. backgrounds.
with
greys, silver, pewter, charcoal
and browns, dull purple,
stronger turquoise & blue
+ muted olive greens.

possibly
some fire lines drawn in
with dye? and maybe
areas washed in with
dye to supplement
chiffons, organza,
nets.

Lettering –
chunky & simple,
slightly compressed
slightly padded gold kid.

EDGAR

Audrey Walker

The third of a series of working drawings and designs presented by Audrey Walker for
One Thousand Years of Monarchy: *preparatory designs annotated with ideas, proposed*
fabrics and techniques.

For an embroidery on this scale a large frame had to be made. This enabled Audrey Walker to roll the work up and to stitch in particular areas or to see the whole panel from time to time by unrolling it and opening it out. It was so large that she always needed help to stretch the work taut. Parts of the panel were worked separately and then added but, when the work was complete, the frame had to be dismantled to get the panel out through the studio doors. A special stretcher was made onto which the completed panel was finally mounted.

The ground fabric is a 2.44 metre width of cotton canvas which proved to be firm but easy to sew through. Always impatient to begin work in fabrics and threads, Audrey Walker drew directly onto the canvas, keeping the cutting of paper patterns to a minimum. A wide range of fabrics from furnishing fabrics to linens, chiffons and nets are used to create a free-flowing patchwork of colour and texture to contrast with the work in gold. Notice the way she uses the transparency of nets and gauzes like water colour washes to create soft patches of colour (*stitch sample 1*). In places these are overlaid to achieve a variety of tones, whilst fragments of dyed lace or knitted fabrics are used to give more opaque crusty areas. The fabrics were cut and tacked into place, then stitched with **herringbone** by hand. This was such a tedious and time-consuming task that Audrey Walker enlisted the help of her friends.

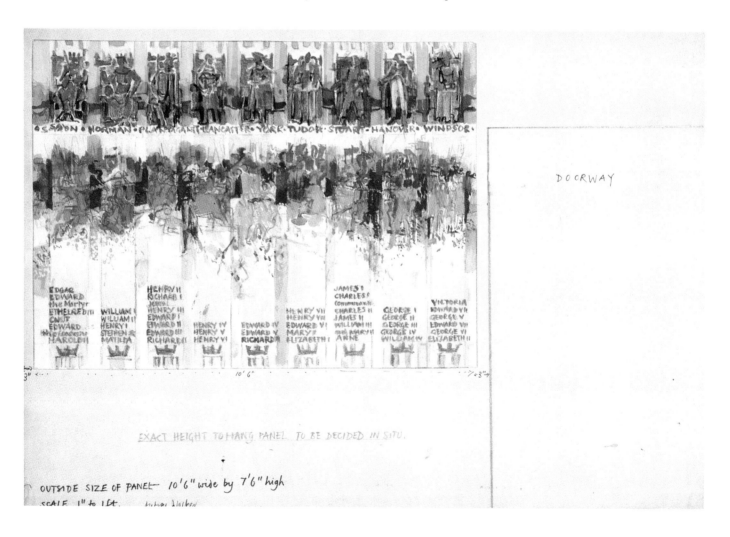

The fourth of a series of working drawings and designs presented by Audrey Walker for **One Thousand Years of Monarchy**: *drawing of the resolved design idea.*

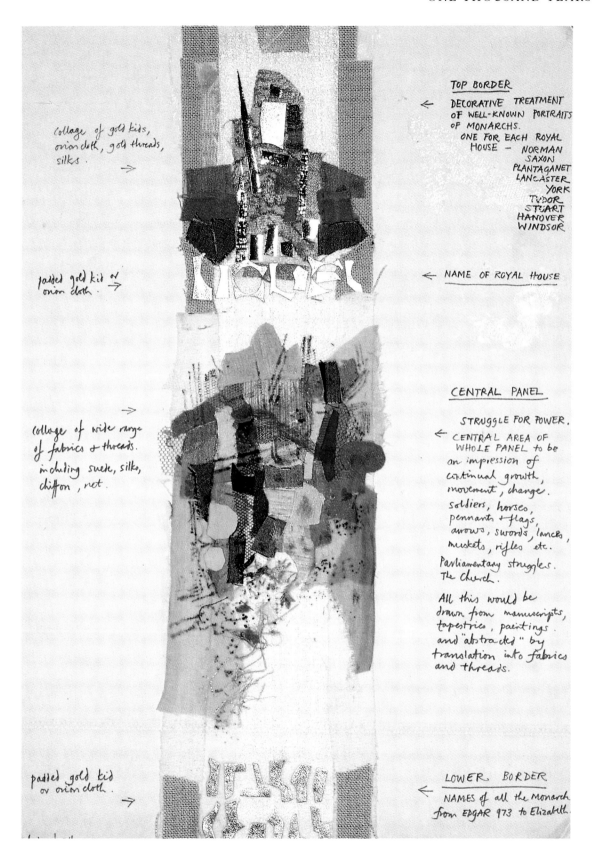

collage of gold kids, onion cloth, gold threads, silks. →

padded gold kid or onion cloth. →

collage of wide range of fabrics & threads. including suede, silks, chiffon, net.

padded gold kid or onion cloth. →

TOP BORDER

← DECORATIVE TREATMENT OF WELL-KNOWN PORTRAITS OF MONARCHS.
ONE FOR EACH ROYAL HOUSE — NORMAN
SAXON
PLANTAGANET
LANCASTER
YORK
TUDOR
STUART
HANOVER
WINDSOR

← NAME OF ROYAL HOUSE

CENTRAL PANEL

STRUGGLE FOR POWER.
← CENTRAL AREA OF WHOLE PANEL to be an impression of continual growth, movement, change. soldiers, horses, pennants & flags, arrows, swords, lances, muskets, rifles etc.
Parliamentary struggles. The Church.

All this would be drawn from manuscripts, tapestries, paintings. and "abstracted" by translation into fabrics and threads.

LOWER BORDER
← NAMES of all the Monarch from EDGAR 973 to Elizabeth.

The fifth of a series of working drawings and designs presented by Audrey Walker for
One Thousand Years of Monarchy: *preparatory selection of fabrics and techniques.*

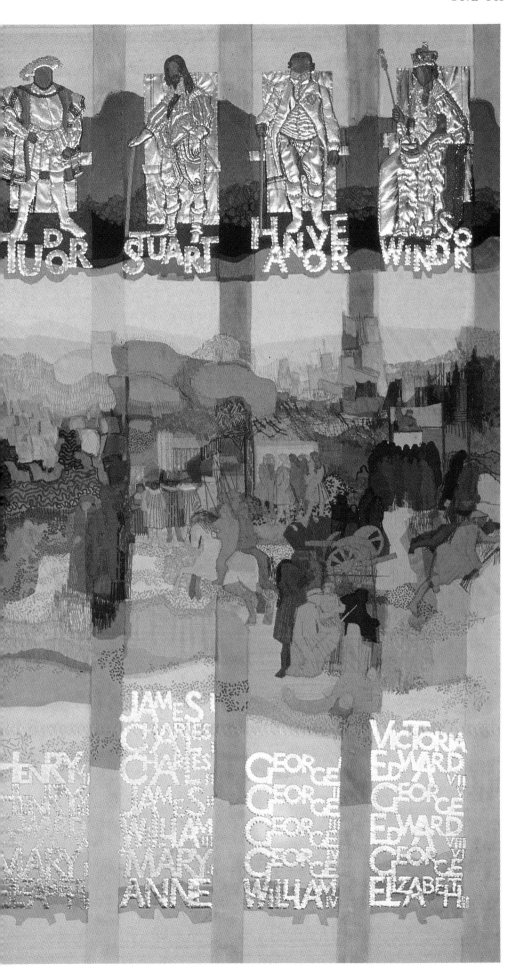

One Thousand Years of Monarchy
Audrey Walker 1973
Commissioned by the City of Bath to hang
in the Pump Room 2·29m × 2·9m.
By permission of Bath City Council
(photo: Unichrome, Bath)

All the stitches she uses are simple. **Seeding** and **knots** are worked mainly in the foreground, but also to reinforce a sense of movement. Blocks of **cretan**, **herringbone** and **straight stitches** are worked like a series of long brushstrokes. Marks in thread have a great advantage over marks made in paints or crayons in that it is easier to make light marks on a dark ground. The extent to which Audrey Walker exploits this became apparent when I studied her work through a series of coloured drawings (*research drawing*).

In an article on the piece, she wrote that one of her difficulties was to keep an overall unity whilst at the same time enjoying the intricacies of the stitches. The figures could have easily dissolved into an abstract flow of pattern. In the central panel, given the freedom to stitch which she so obviously enjoyed, she might have worked across the strips and lost sight of her initial source of inspiration. All the vertical gaps between the strips, however, are worked in darker fabrics and threads, to ensure that the battles are seen as if through a gauze. The banner idea is maintained by an illusion of hanging fabric. The nine strips seem weighted at the top by the solid blocks of gold, but the lettered lists give way to tattered edges at the bottom, thereby strengthening this image.

(a) **Straight stitching**

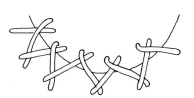

(b) **Herringbone** to apply fabrics

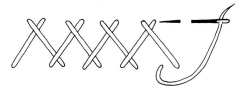

(c) **Straight herringbone**

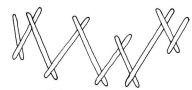

(d) **Free herringbone**

(e) **Cretan**

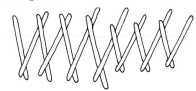

(f) **Cretan** worked freely

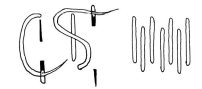

(g) **Slipped cretan**

(h) **Half cretan**

(i) **Seeding** and **speckling**

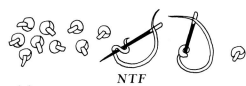

NTF

(j) **French knots**

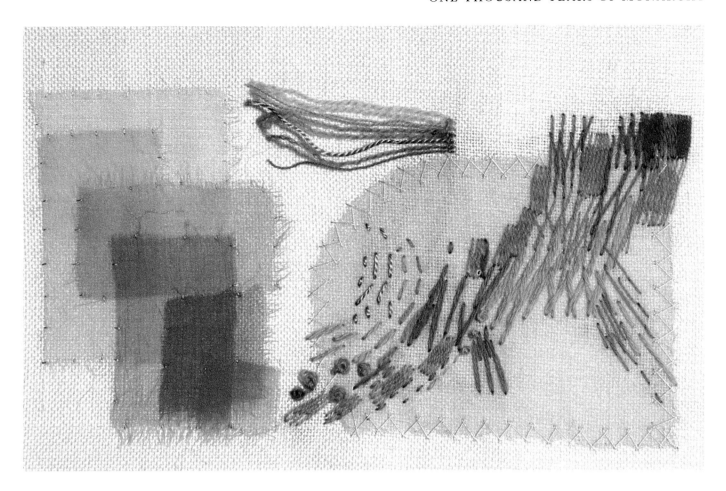

(i) *Transparent fabrics applied by hand to provide soft colour washes and changes of tone*

(ii) *Blocks of* **cretan, herringbone** *and* **straight stitches** *worked to look like a series of long brush strokes with* **seeding** *and* **knots** *to reinforce the sense of movement. The density of the stitches and the colour of the thread both bring about changes in tone.*

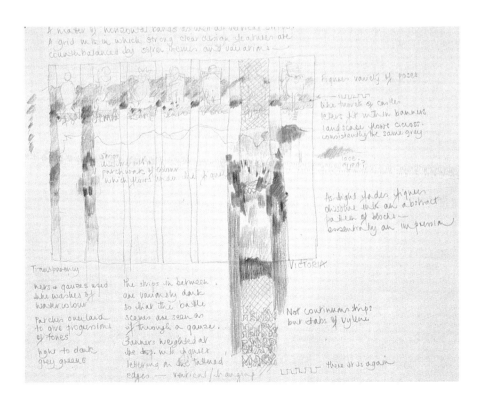

Research drawing *An old gentleman watched me making this drawing. After a while he asked if I was taking down a pattern. He was most surprised when I replied that this was my way of looking at the embroidery more carefully! The drawing is by no means an accurate description. It is out of proportion, extended in ways which reflect the sequence of my observations and littered with written notes.*

Eugenia's Lemon Tree

AUDREY WALKER

The place is a village on the Peloponnese in Greece. Eugenia is a neighbour. From the balcony of her Greek home, Audrey Walker looks down into Eugenia's courtyard with its huge, very prolific lemon tree. On every visit Eugenia is there to greet her and merrily offers her lemons.

Many of Audrey Walker's embroideries evolve from detailed drawings and paintings of landscape and related themes. In this case, before embarking on the piece, Audrey made just a tiny impressionistic sketch which was more of a memory than a working drawing. As well as drawing on the world around her she includes elements of, and makes reference to, the world of textiles. She evokes an atmosphere and conveys a sense of place by working as directly as possible with fabrics and threads. This involves stitching by hand or machine, cutting and piecing, re-stitching and re-cutting until, by a gradual process, she assembles what she wants to express. Nevertheless, her fine art training is always evident in the structure of her work and her approach to drawing and colour.

In 1975 she became head of the textiles department at Goldsmiths' School of Art, London. From her experience there she developed the view that embroidery techniques *per se* are subordinate to the building of a visual language. The visual character of fabrics, threads and stitches are the words through which ideas can be expressed and they far outweigh any importance traditional forms may have had in the past.

Compositions which rely on a square often recur in her work. *Eugenia's Lemon Tree* is square. A central picture is surrounded by a series of strips which imply the architecture of the landscape in which Eugenia is placed. The joins in these strips appear as 'tabs'. At first these suggest a reference to patchwork. This is reinforced by lines of stitching often associated with quilting, but these tabs play an important part in the structure of the composition. If you look across the whole embroidery you will see that the 'tabs' relate to the ground plane on which the flower pot is placed, and to the shutters, and to the tree trunk, and to the figure of Eugenia herself. The 'tabs' also, by extension, integrate the central picture with its more abstract borders and ultimately the wooden frame, which is daubed with colour as were those favoured by Impressionist painters (*photo detail 1*).

Photo detail 1

Eugenia's Lemon Tree *Audrey Walker 1990*
90cm square, including the frame
Collection of Wendy Davis (photo: Dudley Moss)

Photo detail 2

Photo detail 3

When looked at from top to bottom, the central picture in the composition is divided by four unequal vertical bands of colour. The yellow band is particularly intense. It provides the source of light. Any imbalance this might cause is controlled by the narrowness of the band and is counterbalanced by the strips opposite. These contain lesser amounts of the same yellow, as if to reflect the light back. This device is used throughout the work to create sunlight and shadow (*photo detail 2*).

So much for the frame and the composition's structure. What about the picture itself? It evokes the atmosphere of a place at a certain time of year. Eugenia steps out of the shade of the tree to offer a lemon. Audrey Walker has chosen to express a momentary gesture. It is still and hot. The modelling of the figure is subtle. Look at the curve of the hem of Eugenia's skirt and her arms, one in the sun and the other in shadow. The shape of the tree and the depth of the shade feel tangible. The embroidery feels more 'real' than a holiday photograph, but why? (*photo detail 3*)

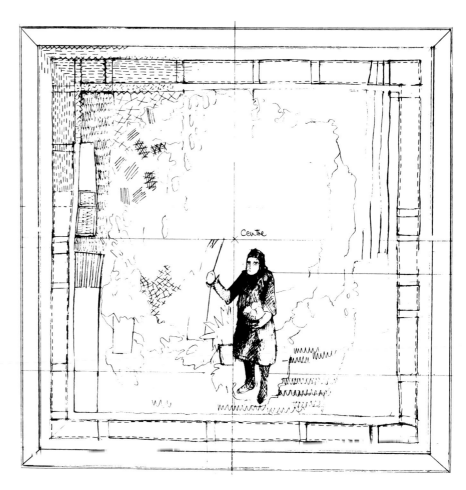

This carefully measured drawing of the embroidery helped me to analyse the underlying structure of the composition.

Throughout the embroidery a fusion of colour, mood and form is achieved by layer upon layer of stitching. Audrey has evolved her own stitch marks which she uses to draw and mix colour simultaneously.

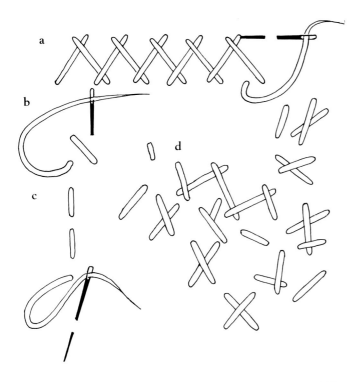

A random form of stitched cross hatching gives an open network of **criss-cross stitches** (d). This is most clearly seen in the shadows. This provides a means of adding colour which allows previous layers of colour to show through. She exploits this to create subtle colour mixes and shifts in tone (photo detail 3).

The cross hatching is broken down into **single crosses** or isolated **slanting stitches**, for example to model the figure, or to create an intermediate texture (photo detail 4) (d).

She only uses conventional lines of **herringbone** to secure applied fabrics and to pattern the borders (a).

Green lines of **running stitch** are paired with pinkish brown all round the border. As these stitches pass through different coloured backgrounds their colour appears to change.

Photo detail 4

Photo detail 5

She has stitched this embroidery as one would paint or make a drawing. This usually involves working quite generally across the whole composition to establish foundation colours and the position of elements in the design. Visual connections are then found and reinforced, and focus is given to images by adding colour and marks. The final phase is usually the slowest and most difficult of all. Often the last stitches are just a few isolated dots of contrasting colour strategically placed to complete the image (photo detail 5).

Subtle variations in tone and colour can be created by stitching a series of open nets of colour one over another.

Red Kite

NICOLA HENLEY

Nicola Henley studied drawing in Florence before taking a foundation course at Bristol Polytechnic. She gained a first-class honours degree in embroidery/textiles from Goldsmiths' College, London, in 1984. Audrey Walker was then Head of Department.

On the Goldsmiths' course an exploration of hand- and machine-embroidered techniques at first led Nicola Henley towards an interest in fragile, disintegrating old costumes. Then she was quick to see that silk screen printing opened up the potential for working on a large scale and for creating images which appear flattened, stacked or floating. When she discovered discharge printing methods she began to combine printing and painting on heavy cotton to re-create the qualities of old cloth. But following a trip to the Ornithological Observatory on Cape Clear in southern Ireland, a long-held interest in birdwatching ultimately became her source of inspiration.

Nicola Henley now creates wall-hung textile pieces from field studies of birds in their natural habitat. Through her work she aims to capture a sense of space and patterns of movement, and to evoke the atmosphere of a place with the character of a bird in its setting.

She seems to be able to transfer the salient elements of these studies and the quality of her drawing in a very direct way through the marks she makes in print and stitch. *Red Kite* evolved from watching kites wheeling over some wooded cliffs in the Alps. It demonstrates her use of marks and colour to create a sense of space, rather than to represent actual depth. For example, the red and gold and white on a background of sombre greys brings the Kite startlingly forward. The offset repeats of the image, first as a red outline and then as a series of marks, reinforce this spatial illusion and add to the sense of movement. These effects belong to the process of printing.

Red Kite Nicola Henley 1988
2m × 2m
Private collection
(*photo provided by Nicola Henley*)

Untitled 1
NICOLA HENLEY

Untitled 1   *Nicola Henley 1984*
approx. 1·5m × 2·5m
Private collection (photo: Dorothy Tucker)

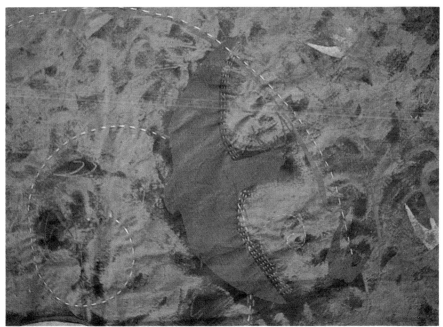

Detail of Untitled 1

Untitled 2

NICOLA HENLEY

From an unusual eighteenth-century gazebo in a walled garden on the outskirts of Bristol, she observed the way in which Jays, Sparrowhawks and Kestrels have adapted to city life. Occasionally she makes drawings from a balloon to help her compose designs based on the perspective of a bird in flight. She now works from a stone barn in the heart of County Clare where the birds around Lough Derg are a constant source of inspiration.

The scale of her work helps to express the freedom of birds moving through space. *Untitled 2*, a large piece some two and a half metres long by a metre and a half wide, illustrates the way in which the key elements of flight patterns are conveyed by symbolic marks as on a map. This piece uses an abstract format to present several flight patterns simultaneously from different viewpoints.

Untitled 2   Nicola Henley 1984
approx. 2m × 2m
Private collection (photo: Dorothy Tucker)

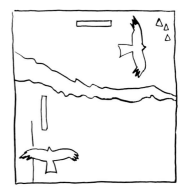

The detail shows how she exploits the way **running stitch**, slightly drawn up, creates an area of tension in the surface of the fabric. This is used to enhance the sense of movement. She heightens the sense of aerial space by contrasting areas of texture with the printed surface. These textures are built up by the trapping down of a variety of materials such as threads, paper, silk or previously printed fabrics with free machine stitching. The richness of these areas is enjoyed most when seen close to.

It could be argued that this is not embroidery; that Nicola Henley uses fabric and threads only as materials for 'art'. Her stitching is certainly sparse but never slight. I am always impressed by the strength and simplicity of her work, and interested in the way that she contains the birds within such unusual, often asymmetrical abstract compositions. Her work is subtle and imaginative, but also always a convincing description of specific birds and their habitat.

She writes:

> I sometimes feel that the way I work attempts to break down the historically evolved division between fine art and craft. I try to override the categorisation by using traditional techniques, rooted in the history of printed and embroidered textiles, combined with a loosely fine art approach, with the emphasis on drawing and painting.
>
> Although this has happened unconsciously, I value more and more the freedom from the restraints which might arise if I keep to one discipline. To be able to paint directly onto cloth, as well as being able to use a range of hand and machine embroidery techniques, affords me a great deal of freedom and flexibility.
>
> This two-fold approach has not only enriched my work but also leaves me open to expand in different directions.

(*Embroidery*, vol. 40 no. 2   Summer 1989)

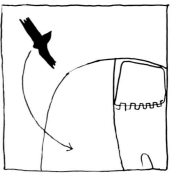

Nicola Henley has had major solo and group exhibitions in Britain and Japan, Ireland and Germany and at the Hothaus Gallery, New York.

All three compositions by Nicola Henley are asymmetrical.

Detail of Untitled 2

A Kantha
BANGLADESH, TRADITIONAL

This is almost certainly a lightweight quilt made for a new-born baby. Rags have been used symbolically in the Indian sub-continent for centuries to deceive the evil eye. Old cloth reworked into another form affirms revival/rebirth. So a Kantha made from a woman's old worn sari has protective qualities and, as far as the baby is concerned, is soft and warm and absorbent. Whilst large quilts are no longer made, women from the rural areas of Bangladesh continue to make Kanthas like these in the traditional way.

This one is faded, with tears and holes in places and cobbled darns. A frayed corner reveals that it is made of a long band of worn cloth with a faded red and blue border running down its length on both sides. The cloth seems to have been folded into four with the ends turned in. **Running stitch** worked with a twisted thread in white, red and two shades of blue has been used throughout.

A Kantha: a lightweight quilt for a newly-born baby. Traditional quilt from Bangladesh 75cm × 99cm
Private collection (photo: Dudley Moss)

In places it seems as if thread of a particular colour has simply run out leaving strange, almost transparent, images. This is probably because materials were scarce and because thread for embroidery was often drawn from the borders of old saris. Many women would hesitate to take thread from anyone but their closest relatives. Some shapes are only partially filled in, or they are stitched in white. These appear void in comparison with the more heavily outlined shapes filled with coloured stitching. Such variations make a design appear to shift in and out of focus.

The preparation of a Kantha is in itself a ritual which involves only married women, usually the mother, grandmother or aunt of the child. The woman first selects the good fabric from a washed worn sari, and then the number of layers required for the thickness she wants. She spreads each piece of cloth and smoothes it out until it is perfectly flat, then adds the next layer. The first stitching, usually in white, runs round all four sides. Once this has been done the work can be picked up and put down at leisure. Then, with running stitch and white thread, the whole surface is marked out in several sections, usually a central square with offsets in all four corners. This phase secures the layers together and provides a working grid. The border patterns are then stitched, first in one colour and then the next. With the cloth in her hands, not in a frame, the woman proceeds to fill the compartments using coloured threads. She works from the centre out towards the edges, and takes the needle through all the layers of sari fabric.

All Kantha designs have a loosely fixed format. There is usually a central lotus flower with open petals (*photo detail 1*). This is embroidered first. Then come the corner motifs which often represent trees and leaves. Around and between these are the figures, animals, and everyday objects that the woman chooses to include. She draws them with her needle, completely free from any need to illustrate things as we actually see them. She fills the outlines with row upon row of running stitch which can distort the fabric and cause some motifs to stand in relief (*photo detail 2*).

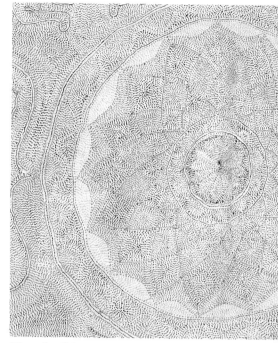
Photo detail 1

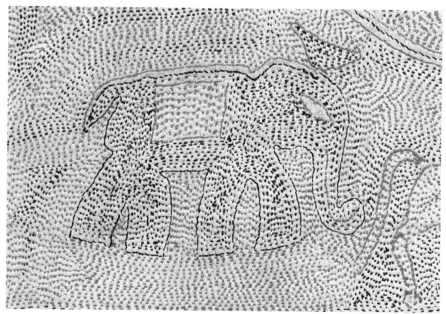
Photo detail 2

Photo detail 3

Finally, when the images are complete, all the remaining spaces are filled with fine quilting, usually in white thread in flowing curves and patterns. Some of the pictures are closely connected with alpanas, the ritual drawings made on the floor with coloured rice flour to mark the changing seasons, a marriage or a birth, etc. (*photo detail 3*).

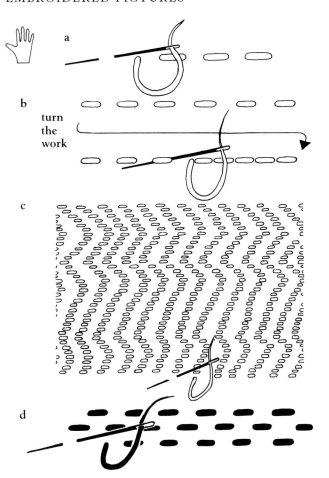

Although a variety of stitches are to be found in Kanthas today, the oldest and most basic are **running** (a) and **double running** (b)

When a Kantha is stitched in order to 'quilt' it, only tiny areas of the cloth are covered. The spaces between stitches are larger than the stitches themselves. Each line of stitching runs parallel to the previous row, but the stitches fall slightly behind or move slightly more forward than those in the row above. It is this stepping which produces the rippled surface. When fine white threads are used on a white ground various quilted patterns are obtained (c).

When thicker coloured threads are used, broken lines of stitching have a speckled look and appear to make ridges of the cloth on both sides of the Kantha (d).

Where the stitches run round motifs and each row comes closer to the centre, they can begin to distort the surface and to cause some areas to stand out in relief. By its very nature, the piece illustrated will never be perfectly flat.

A double row of **running stitch** is often used to outline. This is worked in two stages. First a row of running stitch is made working from right to left. On completing the line the fabric is turned and a second row of running stitch is worked into the spaces of the first, to give a solid line. The thread is taken through all the layers. The stitching is reversible.

A Kantha made as a religious offering or for guests to sit on during a wedding. The compartments round the lotus contain images of the disciples of a guru and symbolic animals at the various levels of spiritual enlightenment.

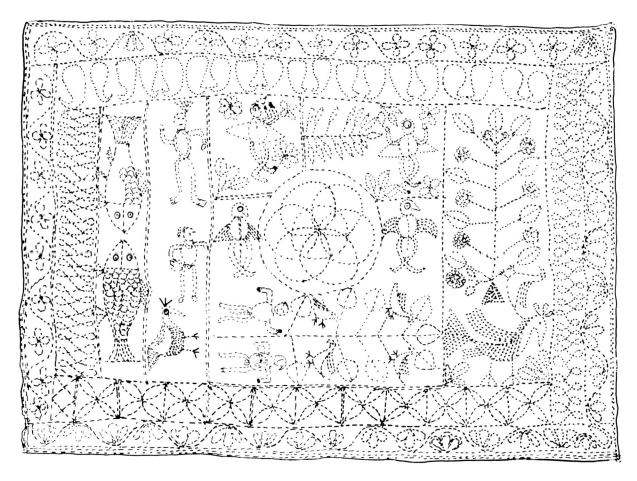

The use of the oldest and the simplest of stitches involves a minimum of wasted thread, and enables work to proceed quickly and fluently. As the woman sews she draws images into cloth, which can be read from both sides, and creates a unique quilted surface. The quilted surface in turn represents the water which is so inextricably part of the life and landscape of Bangladesh. In a place where the rivers support life but also bring floods and calamity, the Kantha maker expresses the flow of the water through the lines of stitching. But look carefully and you will see that these flowing lines are contained within limited areas, or the flow is blocked by a change in direction or colour. Shareen Akhbar in her lectures on the subject says that it is as if the Kantha maker wants to exert some control of the floods she has every reason to fear (*photo detail 4*). The Kantha is made to propitiate the Gods for the well-being of her son-in-law, the safety of her home and children, a good harvest and for the things she most desires.

In March 1988, an exhibition entitled 'Woven Air. The Muslin and Kantha Tradition' opened in the Whitechapel Gallery, London. Many of us found something we were looking for: Kanthas are essentially quilted textiles in construction and purpose, but also art. They are a synthesis of a thrifty, practical use of fabrics and a rural folk art loaded with symbolic meaning.

The Kantha maker simultaneously quilts and draws with her needle. The drawing is free and expressive. Running stitch is the simplest of all embroidery stitches. It is usually the first we learn. When the stitching is complete the Kantha falls into soft folds to cover or to wrap. It is these textile qualities which are being absorbed and taken into contemporary work.

It is interesting to compare these subtle qualities with the clarity of Vanessa Stanfield's *Kantha Cat*. Although both examples employ the same technique, each belongs to a quite different tradition which is reflected in the approach to drawing. The Bangladeshi Kantha is abstract and symbolic. Vanessa's cat is descriptive.

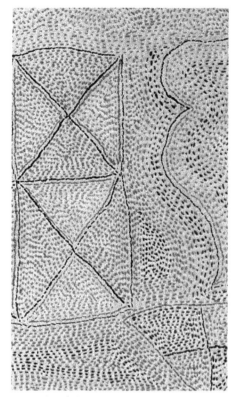

Photo detail 4

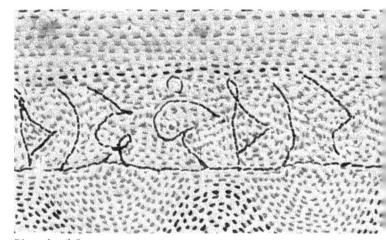

Photo detail 5

The text embroidered in a rural dialect round the borders of the Kantha contains the names of objects associated with good omens, such as a fan for winnowing rice chaff, and fruit. The maker expresses in words her longing for her daughter to marry and dreams as she sews of the many guests coming to the wedding and of the large steel plate full of sweet rice or sweetmeats. She writes her daughter's name and wishes her well.

A Kantha from East Bangladesh made as wrap: white ground with central lotus, floral border, flowers, fish and animals designs stitched in red, yellow, green and black. (Late nineteenth century; the Indian Museum of Calcutta.)

Kantha Cat

VANESSA STANFIELD

Vanessa Stanfield gave *Kantha Cat* to a friend on her birthday. The cat was drawn from a photograph onto the top layer of four layers of sari muslin with a 2H pencil and outlined in **running stitch** taken through all the layers. The tabby markings are conveyed by rows of running stitch in different colours which fill the shape and give it form. The glossy thread used catches the light as it runs through the soft cloth.

The background is divided into patterned zones and stitched white thread on white to give the dimpled quilted surface which had so impressed Vanessa when she saw the Kanthas at the Whitechapel Gallery exhibition. A simple border completes the piece which she has chosen to leave unmounted. Except for the tiny knots and end threads on the back, the work is reversible.

Vanessa found sewing the *Kantha Cat* so rhythmic and satisfying to work that she has stitched a sequel, a circular tablecloth with cats round its border. As she worked on this, she found that she could stitch the cats without following a pencil drawing, and that she became less concerned with detailed markings and more interested in the use of abstract patterns. It is interesting to compare her cat with the horses and elephants of the old Kantha.

Kantha Cat   *Vanessa Stanfield 1990*
23·5cm × 19cm
Private collection (photo: Dudley Moss)

Kantha Cat Tablecloth

VANESSA STANFIELD

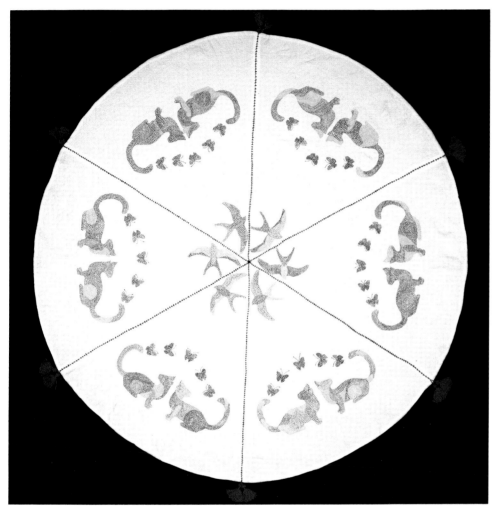

Kantha Cat Tablecloth
Vanessa Stanfield 1992
108cm diameter
Private collection
(photo: Dudley Moss)

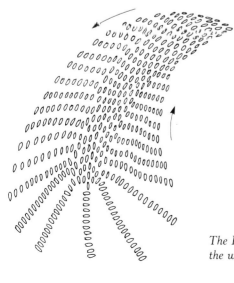

*The Kalka, or Paisley pattern, has been incorporated in
the white stitching of the background.*

Women and Children III

JEAN DRAPER

Since her first textile study tour of India in 1986, Jean Draper has used Indian sources for her embroidery. She first became intrigued by coloured lines of stitching when she saw some quilts from Gujarat. This interest and subsequently an appreciation of the Kantha tradition prompted her to work with the cloth in her hands rather than stretched taut on a frame. She has always found close contact with textile surfaces and stitching by hand exciting and satisfying in themselves.

During a second visit to India, she made a diary sketchbook as she travelled and, of course, took many photographs. She observed people, especially groups of women. As she drew them with their children, the patterns and colours of their clothing seemed to merge and glow.

On her return, she discovered that **running stitch**, worked into a background of felt and layers of fine cotton, gave her the means to interpret figurative images without forfeiting the floral decoration and patterns which so abounded on the fabrics the women wore. There was an added pleasure in being able to depict groups of women and children in the same kind of stitches as they might have used for their own embroidered textiles.

Women and Children III Jean Draper 1991
19cm × 18cm unframed
Private collection (photo: Dudley Moss)

Studies of Indian women selected by Jean Draper from her 'Impressions of India'

In a Kantha the lines of stitching are always worked side by side whether to draw, to add colour, to pattern or to quilt. Jean Draper uses **running stitch** not as a line but as a series of marks which can be varied in size, angle or colour to make patterns or mix colour. She has built the figures by superimposing stitched layers of colour and pattern as well as by working lines side by side.

This is an interesting extension of running stitch which is used in the quilts and kanthas in an essentially linear way.

The panel is so heavily embroidered that at first I failed to see that Jean Draper had carefully placed scraps of fabrics on a foundation of coloured hand-made felt to establish the main shapes of the figures. As I stitched I found that the embroidery was not simply blue, then pink, then orange, etc. as the sequences of my drawings suggest. She often re-threads a colour and works back into a block of stitches, and so the order in which the colours are stitched varies from patch to patch.

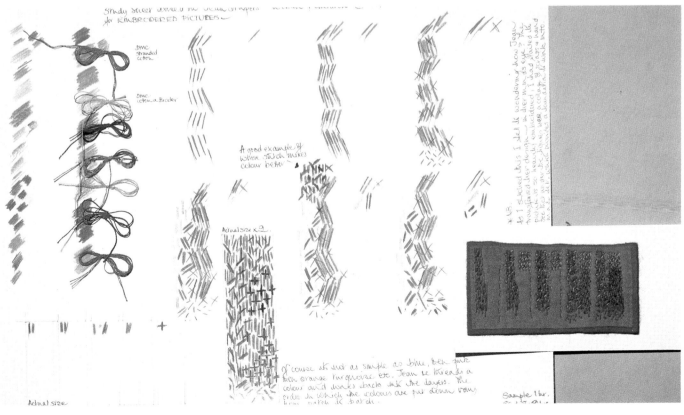

Boston Fishing Lady

NEW ENGLAND, 1745—55

In Colonial America during the seventeenth and eighteenth centuries sewing was basic to every young woman's training. A woman was expected to be able to make and mend clothing and household linen. She learnt to sew from her mother and the older women around her. As she stitched she would have listened to their talk and absorbed their attitudes and role expectations. The assumption was that a woman must marry. From a very early age girls were brought up to be docile, virtuous and obedient, and encouraged in those traits which were to make them good wives and contented homemakers. Girls grew up expecting to run a household but they wanted to marry well. In order to be well regarded they invested many years in becoming skilled needlewomen.

By the eighteenth century wealthy women were able to avoid sewing altogether; after all there were other social diversions open to them such as giving tea-parties and playing cards. However, in a society which valued beautiful

material possessions and fine workmanship, needlework pictures became an important means of displaying female talent.

Some girls learnt to sew whilst they attended a Dame School where pupils could be as young as eight or as old as sixteen and stayed for anywhere between one and three years. In many towns and cities there were needlework schools that gave lessons in, for example, 'colour shading'. From the mid eighteenth century onwards the most successful of these needlework schools also included the teaching of English, French or music, and became the forerunners of Boarding Schools for Girls.

In the seventeenth century samplers were long and narrow, and carried bands of stitch patterns for reference. When they were not being worked from, the samplers were rolled up and put away with the sewing things. In the eighteenth century as samplers became more exclusively part of an educative curriculum and a means of display, they became wider and shorter. By the end of this century they had usually become square or rectangular, and often contained pictures. A simple sampler was often completed in a Dame School. This included initials, or names, and dates in cross stitch and might be a child's first encounter with the alphabet.

Canvaswork was very popular in all the colonies during the seventeenth and eighteenth centuries. This is one of many fine North American needlework pictures known as the Boston Fishing Ladies, believed to have been embroidered by the daughters of prosperous New England families.

Boston Fishing Lady
New England 1745–55
53·34cm × 106·68cm
Henry Francis du Pont Collection,
The Winterthur Museum, Delaware

Photo detail 1

The composition of the picture is such that a series of lines appears to have been drawn across the first two thirds of the canvas to represent the hills. Then selected figures, birds, plants or animal motifs were drawn to fit into the hills as naturalistically as possible despite discrepancies in true scale. Look at the neat feet of the lady with the basket of pears (photo detail 1).

The picture is made up of four distinct bands. The dominant band contains the couples, each scene framed by a pair of exotic trees. Between the trees and settled into the hills are three substantial houses. Initially the difference in scale suggests an attempt to create a sense of distance in the landscape. The houses are more likely to allude to the modest aspirations of the women – placed in the background! Below the couples runs a band of smaller figures in a scale all their own. A gentleman surveys the land from his horse; a commoner walks with his dog; and huntsmen and dogs pursue a stag (photo details 2 and 3). These illustrate manly pastimes. The differences in scale are relative to the importance of the elements in the picture rather than any attempt to represent a real landscape.

The embroidery is on canvas with crewel (see below), silk and accents of metallic yarns. The canvas is much finer than any commonly used today. At anywhere between 22 and 52 holes to the inch, it was excellent for intricate designs. Pictures like this one were stitched almost entirely in **tent stitch**. This was usually worked horizontally, a stitch which without great care could distort a canvas badly. Stitching on this scale required precision and skill. The patience and pride of the makers is reflected in the exceptionally fine work produced.

To colonial women 'crewel' meant fine two-ply loosely twisted worsted yarn. This could be home spun or purchased in different weights from dealers with stocks from England. A woman who lived in Boston, for example, or who had a husband with a business in that city, had access to a wide variety of canvas and of crewel, silk and metallic threads. But in small towns where materials were scarce, countrywomen relied on fabric sales listed in the newspapers for linens and wools from Europe.

Many scenes and motifs for canvaswork pictures came from mass-produced commercial patterns. Engravings published in European magazines provided another source. Copying a superior example was then quite the accepted way of obtaining a well-drawn design. A skilled embroiderer could also turn to a local professional engraver or portrait painter for suitable subjects. In the mid eighteenth century it was fashionable to include one's school building. Popular designs initiated by an art or needlework teacher might be copied again and again. In turn, women borrowed liberally from the needlepoint pictures produced in the Boston Schools. At least sixty-five examples of the Fishing Lady pictures from the Boston Common Group have been recorded and photographed. These records are housed in the Textile Department of the Boston Museum of Art and reflect a fascinating phase in North American needlework.

This particular picture contains three courtship scenes in a rustic setting. A gentleman in a tree picks pears to fill his lady's basket. A maid receives a flower. The lady fishing turns her attention to an admirer dressed in all his finery. The mood is gentle, idyllic and the men are attentive. However, Rozsika Parker in her book *The Subversive Stitch* argues that the passive virtuous attitudes of the women contain a sub-text: their sense of propriety depended upon keeping up their guard against assertive suitors and maintaining protocol at all costs.

In her book *Plain and Fancy: American Needlewomen and their Needlework*, Susan Burrows Swan points out that in the 1700s creativity meant something quite different from what it does today. Although the elements of a picture were probably copied from a variety of sources, when it came to filling in the design, the choice of colours and the way it was stitched were open to the embroiderer's personal interpretation. To us this degree of creativity may seem very slight. But another look at the distribution of a limited range of colour reveals just how much thought and skill were required. A complex balance of light and dark shades lock together like a jigsaw. The large-leafed trees take dark green into the light sky. The main figures are light against the greens. Flowers and animals of every kind stand out as light shapes against dark grounds. The sequence of light and dark tones varies in many subtle ways to accommodate light or dark shapes. This is probably what was meant by 'colour shading'. It was learnt as the accepted way of colouring in a landscape.

Canvaswork pictures are still very popular today. Attractive complete kits by named contemporary designers are eagerly purchased and completed. But what do they tell us about women today, and the status of needlework in our society?

Photo detail 3

Photo detail 2

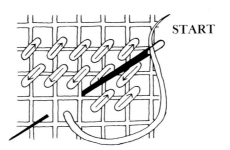

START

Tent Stitch *is one of the most basic stitches in needlepoint, worked horizontally it is also one of the smallest. It is frequently used to stitch fine detail, to make outlines or fill background areas. It is worked over the counted threads of an evenly woven ground fabric, in this case linen, with a blunt tapestry needle. Because both sides of the linen are covered equally well it is hard wearing but worked horizontally it can distort the canvas badly.*

* *Working from right to left, bring the needle out and make a diagonal stitch upwards to cover an intersection of threads. Bring the needle out two threads to the left and one thread down in the hole to the left of the beginning of the first stitch. Continue to the end of the row.*

* *On completing a row insert the needle and bring it out one thread below the insertion point. Turn the work round and continue to the end of the row.*

This sequence is repeated until the required area is covered.

51

Protecting the General

D. R. WAGNER

This artist lives in Sacramento, California. He works in a number of different disciplines: the visual arts, poetry, music and installation. In the mid 1960s he was one of the first Americans to write and publish 'concrete' poetry. His work explores the borders between written and spoken language, sign systems and the visual world of painting. He teaches design at the University of California. Creating miniature canvaswork tapestries is also part of his living and fits into taking a working share of family life.

In the early 1970s, when he was hitch-hiking on sailing boats and island-hopping with his rock group 'The Runcible Spoon' before he came to England, he discovered embroidery. He was without drawing or painting tools but found some floss threads, needle and canvas on board a ship. He was enthralled by the intensity of the colours and the way stitching gave him more control over marks than painting. On reaching England he visited the Victoria & Albert Museum and the Embroiderers' Guild. When he saw the collections of seventeenth- to nineteenth-century work, he decided to make pictures with needle and thread and to use embroidery as a fine-art medium. He tried many different techniques before settling on canvaswork.

Some of Wagner's pictures are about the size of a playing card. He generally uses 25 point cotton congress cloth with four strands of cotton embroidery thread and a no. 24 tapestry needle. A square inch of canvas may contain from between 625 to 1936 stitches. The work is very time consuming and requires great concentration.

Wagner combines in his work ideas and images from many sources, from Grand Opera to comics and pop culture, newspaper items, stories, dreams and personal experiences. He finds juxtaposing different elements a means of discovery, a way of thinking. He says, 'If (an idea) can be expressed in words it will wind up as a poem or story but if it is a visual experience it will most likely surface as an embroidery'. Poem or picture, the source and creative process are the same; only the discipline or product differs.

He writes:

> The process of working with thread is like writing in a number of ways.
> It uses time as writing does. In writing one must make each mark
> clearly to communicate. So it is with canvaswork. One false move and
> the image is changed. The scale is that of writing as well. One can hold
> the work in one's hand. I can introduce change and withdraw ideas.
> Tapestry is another kind of poem.

Wagner wants something to happen when the viewer sees his work. The images must be powerful enough to elicit an emotion or at least to invite questions.

He is aware that exhibitions of paintings can be intimidating, but many people can relate to textiles because 'almost everyone's Grandmother did canvaswork!' It can provide a more familiar and less uncomfortable means of communicating.

In *Protecting the General* a series of action news frames cut from magazines or newspapers seems to run across the canvas, comic strip fashion. A person with a knife is restrained. Two people argue. A face with sunglasses looks out at the viewer. A Samurai draws his sword. Despite the format these frames do not read to tell a story. D. R. Wagner describes them as a series of picture poems. The images feel familiar but seem disconnected. Wedges of primary red and blue, edged with yellow, slice up the action aggressively. Red lines between the arguing couple communicate tension and verbal abuse. Narrow bands of blue

Protecting the General
D. R. Wagner 1985
12cm × 43cm
Private collection
(photo provided by D. R. Wagner)

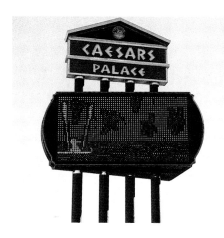

These pictures illustrate both sides of the double-sided electronic signboard designed by D. R. Wagner for Caesar's Palace in Las Vegas. Each board is approximately 6m × 12m, and 7·5m off the ground.

and white indicate locations by the sea. Yellow and black give a sense of strong sunlight. There are many more visual signals, but the overall meaning of the picture remains elusive. What is it about? The embroidery seems to invite more questions than answers.

The canvaswork technique Wagner has developed and his play on images closely connect to the 'pixilated' pictures of video games and computer graphics. It is this division of images into tiny units of colour and light which makes the latest developments in his work possible. The Dectronic starburst double-sided electronic signboard he designed for Caesar's Palace in Las Vegas is a direct extension of his miniature canvaswork pictures. This signboard is 20ft × 40ft, and 25ft off the ground. The 'stitches made in lights' can be seen up to half a mile away. They look very much like canvaswork but have the advantage of changing colour and giving the illusion of movement (*see photos*).

Wagner has more recently begun to use light-reactive paints and fibres. An ultra-violet range is available which gives a whole new dimension to sound and light installations when photographs of his canvaswork are projected.

If these leaps in scale and the use of twentieth-century tools and materials can transform examples of a familiar craft into the visual art forms of the twenty-first century, why do contemporary designs for needlepoint looks so nostalgically back to the past?

Photo detail 1

Photo detail 2

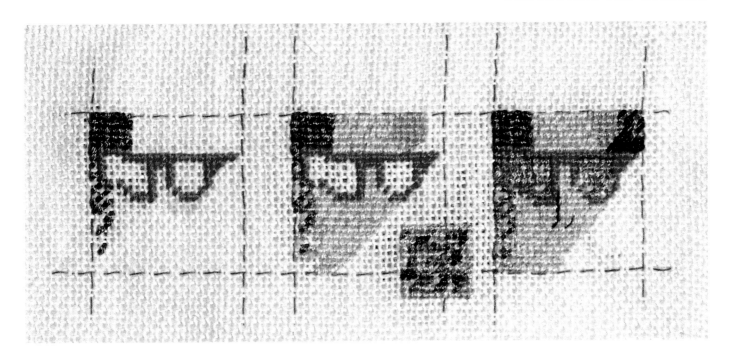

D. R. Wagner's approach to colour mixing is quite different from the colour shading found in the **Boston Fishing Lady**. He selects his threads from a bank of some 600 colours. Choosing a palate may take him several days. It is interesting to find that in **Protecting the General**, as well as black and white and the three primaries, red, yellow and blue, he also uses magenta, turquoise and cyan. These are the colours of light employed by colour film and television. Instead of working bands of carefully graded tones he mixes colour by placing isolated dots or areas of contrasting colours side by side. This creates vibrant, highly-charged colour effects. To achieve this he may have several needles with threads of different colour working at the same time (photo details 1, 2 and 3).

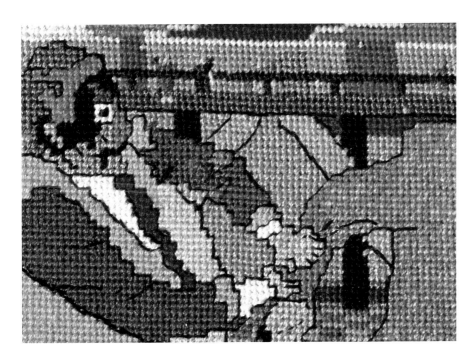

Photo detail 3

Feeding Chickens

SALLEY MAVOR

Feeding Chickens was made by Salley Mavor while she was living in rural central Massachusetts, in an old farmhouse surrounded by cornfields.

The source of her ideas usually comes from 'seeing life happening'. In this case she saw and liked the pattern made by dots of corn fanning out from a woman's hand as she fed her chickens.

The blue sky, the green grass and the house with its path and rose arch are beguilingly elementary. There is no perspective in the picture. The scale of the objects in relation to one another, and the way the space is ordered, feels to be in direct line from the way we drew as children. Salley Mavor's use of stitches could not be more basic or direct. The colour is warm. *Feeding Chickens* is a charming visual poem, tender and wholesome but, above all, uncluttered. The embroidery has a clarity which seems to sing out.

Salley Mavor comes from a very folk-orientated family, and grew up with art, music and dance around her. It was her mother who encouraged her as a child to sew. She is now an artist, illustrator and mother. Her life is full of her young sons and her home but, by swopping time with another young mother, she is able to give time to her work.

Feeding Chickens Salley Mavor 1986
Fabric relief: 61m × 22cm × 2cm
Private collection
(photo provided by Salley Mavor)

(a) Card shape

(b) Wrong side. Woollen fabric glued onto the back of the card shape

(c) Polyester fibre-fill glued onto the front of the card shape

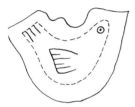

(d) Details embroidered

(e) Wrong side. Fabric secured over card

(f) More details embroidered

(g) Padded shape secured to background

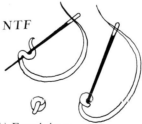

NTF

(h) French knots

After a formal art training she graduated from the Rhode Island School of Design with a degree in illustration. In a department where every sort of art medium was available to her, the only restriction was that she should communicate clearly. Through a slow process of unlearning her formal training, she found her own folk-like style. This began when a tutor suggested she made something the way she had done as a child. This was the beginning of an exploration into soft sculpture techniques. After several years of creating free-standing fabric sculptures, she evolved her two-dimensional relief scenes.

She begins with a simple image which she knows will read clearly from a distance. She then selects and pieces fabrics together to make a background. Sometimes she dyes fabrics (many of them recycled) or sprays them with colour. She enjoys adding borders to set different colours against one another. In the main she uses upholstery fabrics, preferring wools and linens. It was not surprising to discover that she is intrigued by 'stumpwork'.

Some time ago Salley Mavor took text, storyboards and transparencies of two pieces of her work to the Macmillan Publishing Company, New York City. Her book proposal was accepted and Macmillan have published *The Way Home*, a perfect picture book for parents and young children to enjoy together. The simple story was written by Judith Benet Richardson, but it is illustrated with Salley's fabric pictures. She has recently been working on a sequel. Her work photographed as illustration for children's books opens up a world of possibilities for other embroiderers.

The woman and the chickens, the house and the tree trunks are made separately on flat cut-out cardboard shapes (a). A piece of woollen fabric is glued onto the backs of these to give something to stitch into as Salley constructs the work (b). For figures, she usually starts with a body shape and adds on the other sections which have been made separately. This makes the figures more flexible when they are fastened down to the background.

Before Salley 'dresses' a body she glues a small amount of polyester fibre-fill to the front of the cardboard shape (c). Most details are embroidered onto the fabrics before she covers the cardboard cut-outs (d). More may be added once the shapes are dressed or fixed in place (f). The fabrics are secured by a criss-cross of threads on the back of the work (e).

The embroidered features on the background are completed before the figures are attached. But work continues on the figures and the background at the same time in order to relate them to each other. Once the background is complete, Salley stretches it taut across a frame and sews the figures into place. Her husband then constructs a wooden box frame with a glass front to contain the work.

Abraham and Isaac

ENGLAND, SEVENTEENTH CENTURY

It was a great privilege to be able to study the binding of this seventeenth-century New Testament by an arrangement with the Bodleian librarian. The New Testament is housed in a clear perspex box designed by the Curator so that it can be handled and viewed from all sides.

Traditionally the embroidery on the binding was said to have come from the waistcoat of Charles I but, in the Bodleian's view, the existence of several similar bindings and the lack of concrete evidence militate against this idea.

Until the 1770s English booksellers held most of their stock in sheet form. These sheets were bound into books to suit individual requirements. The popularity of embroidered covers was probably due in part to the rarity value of early books which led people to decorate them as precious objects and also to Queen Elizabeth I's interest in embroidery. Certainly a number of books with embroidered bindings were presented to her. Throughout the sixteenth and seventeenth centuries, although many of these bindings were made professionally, many more were embroidered by amateurs. The use of white satin offered an alternative to tooled leathers which had a very strong smell even when masked by a heavy perfume such as lavender. The embroidery was intended to strengthen the fabric and to protect the book as well as to create something which was richly decorative and pleasurable to touch. It was fashionable for Elizabethan and Stuart ladies to hang precious 'treasures', including pomanders and very small books like this one, from their girdles.

In England, during the sixteenth century, girls made their own drawings of flowers and fruit based on herbals. They then embroidered such images, using a relatively limited range of stitches, as floral patterns to decorate their garments and small items of furniture. By the seventeenth century the emphasis had changed to a more marked display of ingenuity and technical skill. This was in part facilitated by the manufacture of finer threads, textured silks and new metallic threads. The maker of this binding had a remarkable range of materials to hand, including white satin, fine floss silks in a range of graded shades, silver and gold threads, a variety of purl (metallic thread) and spangles, the finest of striped silk stockingette, and fine vellum as a support for King David's royal robes.

The embroidered binding has much in common with caskets covered with 'raised work' made in the same period. These were virtuoso technical performances made by young girls who, although freed from the necessity of decorating their clothes, were still required to display their femininity and social status through their embroidery.

The stitching on the front cover near the spine has worn away to reveal that the dog is beautifully drawn in a very fine line of black ink. The quality of the drawing suggests that this may have been done by a professional artist on a prepared background (*research drawing 1*).

An edition of John Taylor's *The Needles Excellency* was available in 1624, the tenth edition by 1631 and the twelfth by 1640. Single sheets of flower prints, animals, birds and Biblical narratives could be purchased from London print-sellers. Some of the flowers and animals are said to be Royalist symbols, e.g. the caterpillar for James I and the butterfly for the Restoration. Designs for the flowers, birds and butterflies which fill the spaces between the figures on this binding could have been chosen and copied straight onto the satin from engrav-

Research drawing 1

ings in the pattern books of the period (*research drawing 2*), or transferred by 'pricking and pouncing' which led to the destruction of printed pattern sheets.

Many items necessary for the construction of pictures like these were available already made up by professionals. An amateur could purchase and skilfully put them together in an arrangement of her own. Both professional and amateur pictures reflect the preoccupations of Elizabethan and Stuart embroiderers. Virtue is implied by the minute scale and perfection of the work, and value by the variety of materials used and the richness of the overall effect.

The story of Abraham and Isaac was a favourite Biblical narrative for embroidered pictures. Rozsika Parker in *The Subversive Stitch* suggests that the constant repetition of this theme, parental power at its most absolute and violent, had a powerful resonance within seventeenth-century families where parents, particularly fathers, were assuming new authority.

Our view of the world is so dominated by images reproduced in books and magazines, newspapers and television, we tend to organise a picture in a single frame as though through the lens of a camera. The composition of the embroidered binding could free us from such a one-frame view of the world. After all, photography has enormous potential for combining a variety of visual images from different sources within the same printed spread. Used in conjunction with photocopiers and computers, photographs are often our source of inspiration and design in just the same way as engravings were to the embroiderers of the seventeenth century.

Research drawing 2

Abraham and Isaac   *17th century*
English embroidered bookbinding   8·5cm × 11·5cm × 2·5cm
The Bodleian Library, Oxford   (Douce Bib. Eng. N.T. 1625 g.1)

The embroidery is not as haphazard as it first seems. It is composed of two main elements. The first is a tableau of figures representing a Biblical story, the feet clearly on the ground and the dress contemporary. The second element, seen in the spaces round the figures, consists of little pictures from the world of flora and fauna. Spangles were then sewn into any remaining spaces. The composition allows the two elements to co-exist quite happily. This peculiar form of construction for a Biblical narrative was perhaps the beginning of pictorial embroidery for its own sake rather than, as it had been, part of furnishings.

Research drawing 3

The frame of King David's harp is filled with needle-lace on a fine gold wire. Look at his collar, cuffs and crown. The work on this minute scale must have been very exacting and time consuming. Tiny pieces of wood and stuffed areas were used to give the figures three-dimensional form.

King David and Abraham are in contemporary rather than Biblical dress. The King is in silks and Isaac simply dressed to signify individual character or role. The folds of King David's robes, flowing from under his lace collar, are most carefully modelled over folded vellum to be as real as possible, as are his hair and crown. The faces of all three characters are skilfully modelled on a padded base covered with directional surface stitching in silk. They look out at us.

Had the embroidery been worked to true scale the flowers and animals would have been so small that their distinctive features would have been lost. The disregard of scale allows an importance to be given to them which reflects the 17th century interest in the natural world. We can see that this is a pansy and that a tulip. The petals of the flowers are wired and coloured to make them look 'real' and identifiable by name. It was during the 17th century that flower gardening and embroidery became more distinctly the province of women.

It is interesting to try to identify the materials used in the 17th century and to match them with materials available to the embroiderer today.

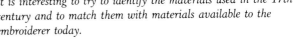

(a) Three different shades of **Maltese silk** *to match and couch metallic threads*

(b) **Floss silks**

(c) **Very fine sewing silk thread**

(d) **Passing** *This is a smooth strong pliable thread available in different thicknesses. It is made from sheets of gold beaten tissue thin, cut into very narrow strips and then coiled round a core of floss silk.*

(e) **Purl** *There are various different types of purl: smooth, rough and pearl purl (also called wire purl or badge purl). Purl consists of gold wire drawn out very finely and then coiled closely together like a spring. It is often cut into short lengths but there are endless ways of using it.*

(f) **Plate** *Plate is a narrow strip cut from a plate of beaten metal.*

(g) **Spangles** *These are made by coiling metal wire round a wooden or metal core. The wound coil is then cut along its length to produce a number of wire rings. These are hammered flat to form discs with a central hole and a side slit. Spangles like these have been made since medieval times.*

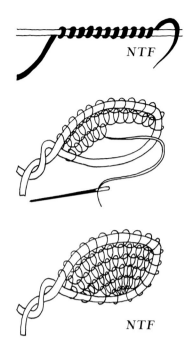

Fine copper wire, wrapped with silk thread, was used to create the petals or leaves of flowers and the wings of butterflies. The wire shapes were then filled with **detached buttonhole** worked in bands of graded colours. These wired shapes stand away from the background. Underneath them the design would be echoed in flat stitchery, usually **satin** or **long and short stitch** (photo detail 1).

Photo detail 2

Figures were made by cutting out shapes in linen which were then stretched over card and padded with horsehair or wool. Paper pasted onto the back prevented the linen from fraying. The embroidered piece was then applied to the background with small slip stitches (photo detail 2).

The faces were carved from wood and painted, or modelled in wax and covered with silk. The features were embroidered on the silk in close satin stitch (photo details 2 and 3).

Photo detail 1

Postscript

Chapter Two of Muriel Best's *Historical and Contemporary Raised Embroidery* provides a fascinating link between this embroidered book binding and the casket which inspired Ann V Sutton's *The Spencers Gardening*. Before it became popular in English domestic embroidery, raised work was extensively used on the Continent for ecclesiastical work.

In 1625, a man called Nicholas Ferrar founded a Christian community in Little Gidding near Huntingdon, England. This included many members of his family. They lived in a manor house on an estate belonging to Mrs Ferrar, his mother, where they restored the derelict medieval church. As well as devoting itself to charitable works, the community prepared harmonies of the scriptures, and produced exquisite needlework and decorative bookbindings. Charles I visited the community several times. Nicholas Ferrar died in 1637 but the community continued until 1642 when the Civil War drove them abroad. When they returned in 1646 they introduced raised techniques in their work, influenced by the ecclesiastical embroidery they had seen on the Continent. This included their decorative book bindings.

When the Puritans discovered that the community had provided Charles I with a sanctuary, soldiers desecrated the chapel and the manor house, and the community was dispersed. Only the chapel still remains. This has been restored again by a new Christian community.

Photo detail 3

The Spencers Gardening

ANN V. SUTTON

There are certain things we go back to see in a museum because they are a special source of pleasure and inspiration. For Ann Sutton this is a collection of needle-work made by Martha Edlin displayed in the Victoria & Albert Museum, London. The collection is unique because all the work belongs to one person. Some items, clearly worked under tuition, are to be seen alongside pieces reflecting a more personal choice and interpretation. Amongst her beautifully worked band samplers there is a casket covered with **raised work**. Dated 1671, this took two years to complete. The side panels, illustrating scenes from the Old Testament, are embroidered with silk threads on linen with **tent stitch**. They are further decorated with detached buttonhole silk cords and purl (metallic thread). Each time Ann Sutton saw this she became more intrigued by the techniques employed. When a practical course on 'raised work' techniques was advertised she seized the opportunity to extend her interest.

The Spencers Gardening is based on a postcard of a detail from one of Stanley Spencer's paintings. As soon as she saw it, the postcard evoked her childhood. She had lived in the country in a flint-built cottage where Uncle George, who always wore a hat and leather gaiters, tended the vegetable garden and her Aunt Peggy grew flowers. She had helped to pull carrots in the summer; the apple tree provided bunches of mistletoe every Christmas.

The postcard brought back memories of being a little girl sitting amongst the pea-poles watching her aunt and uncle at work. Stanley Spencer's positioning of the figures is exactly as she remembers their working together. Spencer's deliberate distortion of the man to express his presence accords with Ann's great fondness for her uncle. Because Spencer's figures are faceless, Ann Sutton was able to transfer her own identity to them. The tweedy hat hides her uncle's face, the old blue straw her aunt's smile.

Although copying the figurative work of a great English painter, Ann Sutton has so infused his composition with her feelings that she has transposed his picture into something of her own. The postcard gave her an initial design on which to show her mastery of three of the four raised work techniques. She has used layers of brown felt to pad the figures. Uncle George's hands are wired. On Aunt Peggy's jacket the **buttonhole stitch** is openly spaced over a brown felt pad to give a tweedy look (*stitch diagrams j and h*). Another variation over pink felt for her skirt allows a hint of colour to show through (*stitch diagrams h and i*). This is echoed in the ribbon round her straw hat. The ribbon gives the picture a focal point. Another variation of buttonhole, very closely

The Spencers Gardening
Ann V. Sutton 1984
18cm × 13cm
Private collection (photo: Dudley Moss)

worked on a cordonnet, suggests the weave of the basket (l). The basket was made separately and then applied, as was Uncle George's hat. The spaces surrounding the figures are then filled with surface stitchery to create the garden plants. The stitches used include **fly** (f), **raised needle weaving** (k), and **banksia rose** (a to e).

In many ways, this embroidery adds up to a demonstration piece, a sample picture which puts into contemporary form techniques gleaned from seventeenth-century examples of raised work. When she created this, Ann Sutton was learning. *The Spencers Gardening* is a direct result of attending a class. Ann Sutton is now an embroidery teacher in her own right. From time to time she shows the picture to her students to illustrate technique or to develop their interests and sources of inspiration. This is a powerful way of conveying skills and an enthusiasm for embroidery. Perhaps as well as an interest in technique, women in the seventeenth and twentieth centuries share a need to create ingenious small-scale treasures, with no function other than to absorb time in pleasurable invention. Ann Sutton's picture is framed in a clear perspex box frame to hang on a wall. Our equivalent, perhaps, to the precious items hung from the girdles of Elizabethan and Stuart ladies?

BANKSIA ROSE

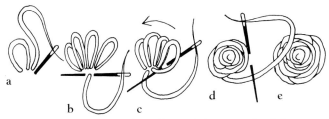

The stitch used to create the cabbages is known as *banksia rose*.

* First make a small loop no more than 0·4cm high (a). Work three more loops the same size and close together to form the centre of a rose (b).
* Bring the thread out near to the loops by making a small stitch on the back. This will help to keep the loops secure (b).
* Then, moving anti-clockwise, work some long stem stitches round the centre, leaving the loops as loose and as high as though in the middle (c).
* Keeping an even tension and working the stitches close to each other, continue to encircle the centre but gradually reduce the height of the loops so that by about the fourth round they are almost flat (d). The 'petals' should appear to enfold one another (e).

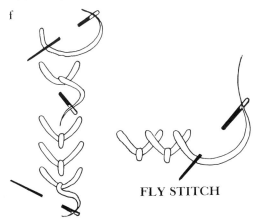

FLY STITCH

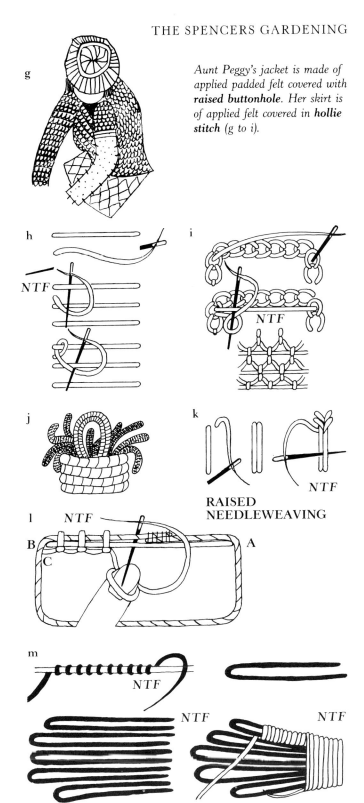

Aunt Peggy's jacket is made of applied padded felt covered with **raised buttonhole**. *Her skirt is of applied felt covered in* **hollie stitch** *(g to i).*

RAISED NEEDLEWEAVING

Uncle George's hands are made of wire wrapped with thread. Each finger is separate and curled round the handle of his spade (m).

* Bind a separate piece of wire with thread for each finger or thumb. Bend each wire over to the desired length, i.e. a finger's length plus the length of the palm.
* From the base of four fingers and a thumb, bind round all the doubled wires to represent the palm of the hand. Then bind each finger and the thumb separately.
* To fasten off, return to the base and take the end of the thread into the bound palm.

The Magic Garden

REBECCA CROMPTON, 1934

In the days when a book could carry only one colour illustration, Rebecca Crompton chose *Magic Garden* to partner the title page. The caption reads:

> A design worked in **appliqué** by direct methods. It shows the use of superimposed stitchery across the form, rather than the emphasis of outline. Pattern and plain materials are used. **French knots** give richness to the background.

One can almost hear her teaching voice! The piece illustrates many aspects of her innovative approach. The purples, reds, pinks, oranges and greens are Mrs Crompton's colours.

Her interest in the content of this picture is slight in comparison to her interest in the use of fabrics and stitch. The piece is about design and flat areas of pattern rather than any attempt to re-create reality or to express feelings.

All the elements in the design either overlap or are linked by her distinctive looping lines. The face is within a circle which overlaps a double circle. The circles frame the figure. Some of the circles and shapes are applied cut-outs from plain and patterned fabrics. Other shapes and circles are created by areas of stitching or areas void. The stitches are simple and direct. Throughout the work, the tonal contrasts, both in colour and texture, are typically sharp and strong. It is a surprise to find that the embroidery is stitched entirely in blues, greys, black or white, except in the circle round the face. This startling discovery provides a simple and effective approach to combining patterned fabrics with a range of embroidery stitches. This embroidery travels across shapes and patterns in a way which reminds us that embroidery need not be only concerned with drawing outlines or providing detail in a descriptive way.

Rebecca Crompton was born in 1895. She was a student at the Derby School of Art at the beginning of the 1920s. By all accounts she was a lively, dynamic personality. She was very fond of brilliant combinations of reds, purples and pinks, and jade green. By the 1930s, she was a very influential teacher of dress design and embroidery. Her strikingly innovative clothes impressed her students. Her approach was an extreme swing away from traditional design and techniques. One of her students remembers being nonplussed when she was asked to interpret one of Rebecca Crompton's scribbled drawings in class. To begin with, she had no conception of what she was supposed to do! Another student remembers rebelling against Mrs Crompton's preference for vivid colours by working a piece entirely in browns!

In England, Rebecca Crompton showed her work in various exhibitions. During the 1930s she pioneered mixed-fabric techniques. Appliqué with surface stitchery became a favourite means of interpreting flat areas of colour and patterns for contemporary designs. She combined plain with patterned fabrics, incorporated lettering and used a variety of textured and transparent fabrics together. Her inclusion of raw edges horrified conventional embroiderers, who criticised her work for being carelessly executed. Her breakaway from traditional rules helped to free embroidery from the rigid outlook of the early part of the century. It was this freedom to mix fabrics and techniques which led to an interest being taken in embroidery as art by artists. She also pursued the possibilities of machine embroidery for contemporary designs by going to Dorothy Benson at the Singer Workrooms.

The Magic Garden
Rebecca Crompton, 1934
52cm × 36cm
Photo by courtesy of the Board of Trustees of the Victoria & Albert Museum, London

66

In 1935, she retired from full-time teaching to work for an exhibition in conjunction with her book *Modern Design for Embroidery*. The editor wrote in the book's Foreword,

> Mrs Rebecca Crompton has shown in her own work, and now shows in this book, how the embroideress may become a creative artist instead of being merely a copyist; how embroidery even in its simplest form, may become the expression of personal thought and feeling; how materials and textures and colours can contribute to the interpretation of design and produce effects unobtainable by stitchery alone.

Rebecca Crompton's aim was to show how embroidery could be studied as a creative craft. In her opening chapter, she begins by saying that creative embroidery is concerned with the relationship of stitchery and design. Instead of attempting to learn a large vocabulary of stitches through working mechanical rows, she proposed that the embroiderer should experiment to discover new possibilities. Only a few stitches should be selected at first. From such experimental variations, much could be learnt about the use of different materials, colours and stitches.

She said that the creative worker should view a drawing as a painter would view a slight preliminary sketch, from which ideas can be developed as the work progresses.

> Embroidery should never look as if it were squeezed out of shape in order to follow a previous conception of correct drawing or illustration. It should direct the right kind of drawing.

Rebecca Crompton's line drawings were spontaneous and carefree. In many of her embroidered pictures she used looped lines to link isolated areas of her designs. This device became a cliché in the work of others and a distinctive feature of embroidery in the 1930s.

She advocated pinning up work in progress and standing back to view it, and the use of paper cut-outs or drawings on transparent paper as ways to develop or change a design. This, she wrote, should lead to a personal interpretation of a drawing, not an exact reproduction. She thought that if the embroidery of flowers and figures were carried out in a lively, playful way, then design would be spontaneous and expressive.

When the book was published in 1936 it caused a great stir. Her experimental outlook was far beyond many traditional embroiderers of her day and revolutionised the teaching of embroidery. Her influence is still evident in contemporary work and good practice today. Contemporary embroiderers expect to work from their own designs and to interpret them with an open experimental approach to stitchery I wonder how Rebecca Crompton would have viewed Audrey Walker's work or Nicola Henley's *Red Kite*.

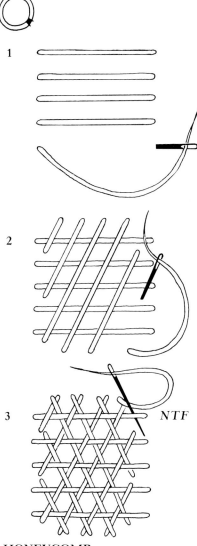

HONEYCOMB FILLING STITCH

The embroidery reproduced in black and white demonstrates the sharp tonal contrasts in Rebecca Crompton's work.

L'Heure bleue

LUCIENNE LANSKI

Of all my books, perhaps *The Constance Howard Book of Stitches*, purchased soon after it was published in 1979, is the most battered through use. Mainly in black and white, it illustrates a series of one-stitch variations. These are worked to encourage an experimental and free approach to familiar embroidery stitches. It demonstrates how the use of different threads, changes of scale, even or uneven stitching, can change the look of a stitch. It shows how to alter stitches simply by varying the angle of the needle and the way in which new stitches can be invented. It is a unique reference book because the stitch samplers clearly relate more to mark making and drawing than to traditional embroidery techniques. No interpretations are given. Embroiderers are challenged to explore the scope and versatility of stitches, and encouraged to find their own style of stitching to express their own ideas in a lively and original way.

It was in June 1984 at an International Festival of Embroidery at Clarendon Park, Salisbury, that I first saw Lucienne Lanski's *L'Heure bleue*. I have never seen **buttonhole stitch** worked with such freedom and spontaneity. By adapting, moving and changing just one stitch, she has evolved a very direct form of drawing which she uses to express both mood and form. The lacy patterns created by the rhythm of her stitching suffuse the scene with a dream-like quality. The three women seem to emerge and dissolve into a fantasy of flowers and dappled light. Their attitudes and clothes belong vaguely to the past. The mood is gentle and reflective.

I was intrigued as to how Lucienne Lanski had come to such a fluent and original way of stitching, and was later able to attend a lecture she gave on her work. Listening to her I was struck by the fierce all-consuming energy with which she spoke about her embroidery. She lives in Paris. She is first and foremost a writer of fairy tales and poems, but she described how, in interludes between writing, ideas come to her. Then, as if under a spell, she stitches and stitches, drawing upon her imagination until a picture is complete and her energy spent.

She works without a frame and begins by drawing a few essential lines, sometimes in running stitch or even with a ballpoint pen! She always chooses a fabric to give a strong background colour. At first she works with thick cotton threads. In her hands buttonhole stitch becomes an open net of colour. The stitches allow the background colour to show through and the spaces between are open for new possibilities to occur. Later she often fills the net with **knots** or **single chain stitches**. She extends an image by overlaying the work in thick cotton with another network of stitches, using a finer thread. Finally she refines the images using very fine sewing cotton, occasionally adding highlights in silk. By spreading nets of colour one over another in different weights of thread she is able to fuse images together in a most extraordinary way.

Depending on the angle of her needle, the stitching can be quite flat. Worked into itself, it can lead to frilled edges.

She has a tendency to encircle shapes by working and re-working into their edges with a single colour. This can create a strange aura round images; they appear to expand and glow. The effect adds to many of the unreal qualities in her work, well suited to pictures which come from the world of her imagination and not the world around us.

As a child she learnt how to sew at school. Otherwise her art is untutored and self-taught. As a young girl, she was skilled at copying, and used to draw pictures on cards for her family and friends in France.

After the break-up of her marriage she went to Brooklyn, New York, where new artistic friends were so delighted when she used needle and thread to draw a more personal card that they persuaded her to enter a competition at the Brooklyn Museum. She was working at that time in a restaurant. On her way home one evening she found a large piece of black fabric in the street. She picked it up, washed it and, with any threads that came to hand, started stitching. First a shell, then a tree, and from the tree emerged a man, and so on . . . *The Liberty Tree*, as it became, released half a lifetime's emotions and bottled-up creative energy. When this embroidery won an award, Lucienne was exultant. She describes this as the beginning of the beginning of her life as an independent artist.

The urgency with which she works has led to her distorting a stitch learned as a child, transforming it into a highly individualistic style of embroidery. By not losing time in taking out mistakes, but instead covering them over with more stitches, she discovered a whole world of effects and the interaction of colour.

On returning to Paris she studied the paintings of Van Gogh with renewed interest and has subsequently exhibited her work in many parts of the world. She describes her work as 'broderie sauvage' (wild embroidery). On being asked why, she replies,

Parce que c'est une technique de broderie en opposition avec la broderie classique.*

L'Heure bleue   *Lucienne Lanski 1983*
approx. 28cm × 46cm
Private collection
(photo provided by Lucienne Lanski)

*Because it is a technique in total contrast to classic embroidery.

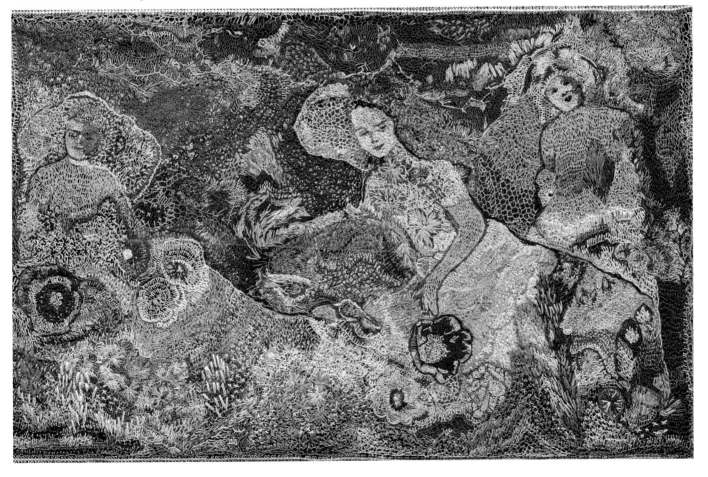

Liberty Tree

LUCIENNE LANSKI

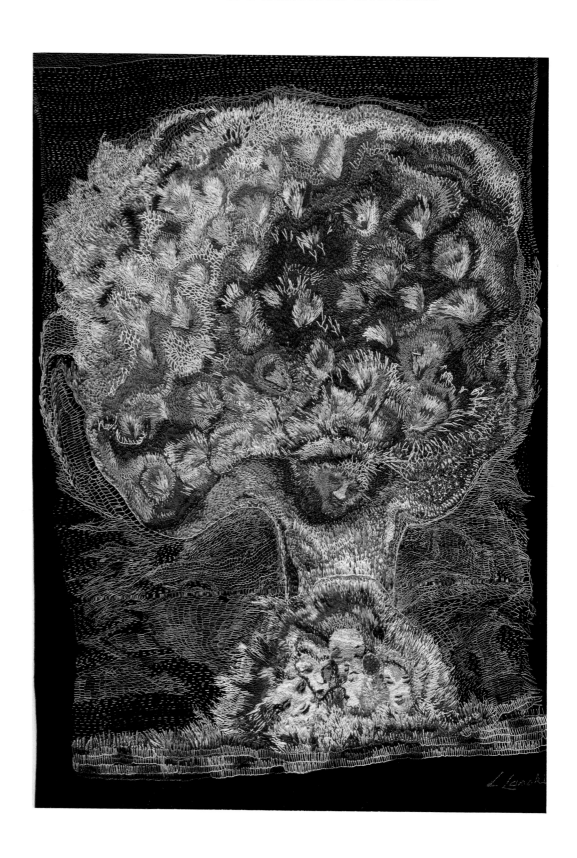

Liberty Tree
Lucienne Lanski 1977
1·20m × 1m
Private collection
(photo provided by
Lucienne Lanski)

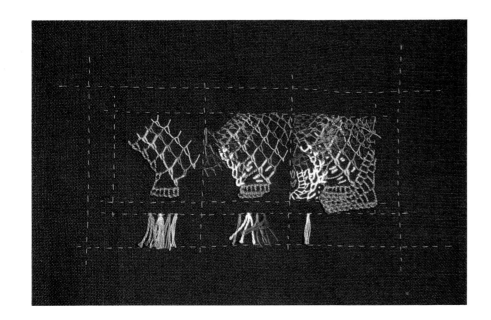

Lucienne Lanski first stitches an open net of colour using a thick thread. She then overlays this with another network of stitches using a finer thread. Finally she refines the image with a very fine sewing cotton.

Later she often fills the nets with **bullion knots** or **single chain stitches**.

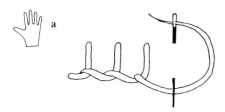

(a) Traditional **buttonhole stitch**

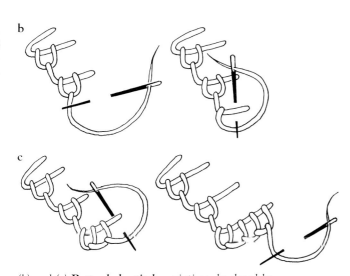

(b) and (c) **Buttonhole stitch** variations developed by Lucienne Lanski

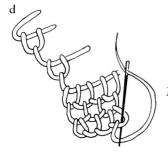

NTF

(d) Worked into itself, **buttonhole stitch** can lead to detached lacy edges.

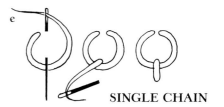

SINGLE CHAIN

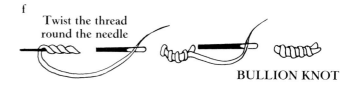

Twist the thread round the needle

BULLION KNOT

A Furisode Kimono
JAPAN, LATE EDO PERIOD

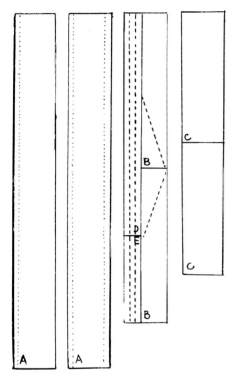

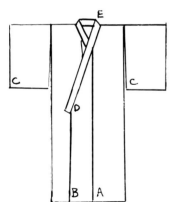

Western clothes are constructed from shaped pieces of cloth often cut and sewn on the bias to achieve 'a good fit'. A kimono, however, is constructed from seven straight rectangles cut from a single bolt of cloth. These are folded and loosely basted together edge to edge so that they can be taken apart for cleaning. Great skill is required to produce a length of cloth with a design the right way up on both the front and back of a kimono. When the pieces are cut and assembled the alignment of the motifs must be perfect.

Kimono designs and styles are so varied that, in order to classify them, they are named after textile techniques, historical eras or the names of people and places. The 'Furisode' style of this kimono is characterised by the long swinging sleeves. By the end of the eighteenth century some sleeves were so long that they touched the ground. The sheer impracticality of this fashion implies a leisured life style or a ceremonial use. Kimonos are traditionally worn with an 'obi', a contrasting sash which is wound round the body and tied in a large knot. The obi designed to partner this kimono is unfortunately not in the Embroiderers' Guild Collection. The perfect condition of the kimono suggests that it has never been worn.

Edo (now modern Tokyo) was a flourishing city in the seventeenth century. Its prosperous merchants and artisans wanted fine clothes and entertainment. At all levels in society the kimono was a vital element in traditional tea ceremonies and weddings as well as status symbols in everyday life. The costumes designed for the theatre and portrayed in the prints of the period were important vehicles for artistic expression. It seems to me that the art of the kimono lies not only in the images conveyed but also in the textile techniques combined to produce them. Stimulated and supported by wealthy patronage, the kimono designers of the Edo period had a wide variety of specialists at hand to spin, weave, dye and embroider.

From 1600 to 1868 Japan was isolated from any outside influences. As China was the only source of fabrics and threads, the majority of Japanese motifs were Chinese in origin. Any new techniques were developed from a study of textiles imported from China or by Chinese textile artists settled in Japan. It would be interesting to trace how such a distinctly Japanese preference for bold colours, discontinuous designs and asymetrically placed motifs developed, and why.

As well as using the natural world as a source for design Japanese artists often included man-made objects in their work. The folding fan is a popular motif, often seen fully open, sometimes closed and at various stages in between. This kimono is scattered with a number of different fan-shaped frames. Each contains an embroidered picture. The courtier on horseback and Karako, a Chinese boy attached to the Japanese court, may illustrate episodes from a well-known story. Other frames contain birds and plants. In a culture where every season has its festivals, each month its special flowers, and the hours and years are given animal characters, these may be significant. Pine or bamboo, for example, symbolise a new year and tortoises (*photo detail*) long life.

A stencil for the fans was probably cut from a heavyweight oiled paper and placed on the fabric. A loose paste would then have been spread over the fan shape and the stencil removed. A very thin sheet of gold leaf was pressed gently onto the drying paste and burnished very lightly to ensure its adhesion and surface quality. The different sponged, speckled and solid areas of gold on this

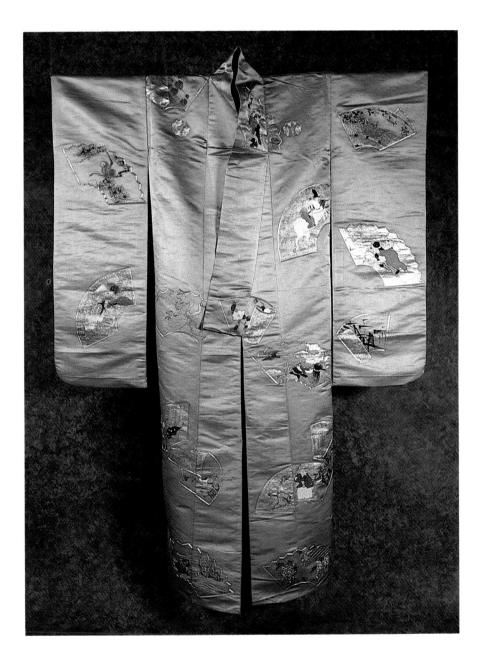

A Furisode Kimono *Japan*
Late Edo Period
162cm long
The Embroiderers' Guild Collection. EG 20.
1984 (photo: Julia Hedgecoe)

kimono suggest that variations could be made in the way that the paste or the gold leaf was applied. This technique, known as *surihaku*, was developed to copy a special loose-weave silk imported from China called *inkin* (stamped gold). This was used for mounting calligraphy and paintings. *Surihaku* is usually associated with relatively inexpensive kimonos because it provided a fast and economical substitute for rare Chinese brocades. Because it seemed so flat and dull in comparison, touches of embroidery were added. At first coloured silks were used and then small quantities of rounded gold threads imported from China. Almost inevitably the embroidery took over until surihaku became simply its background.

A contemporary version of this design could begin from scattered photographs to show, for example, different aspects of a place. What other man-made objects could provide a series of frames for pictures? Although stretch fabrics now enable us to relate design to body shape in the most extraordinary ways, simply-constructed garments such as the kimono still offer perfect formats for surface decoration and picture images.

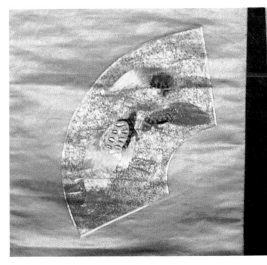

Head of Christ

BERYL DEAN

Beryl Dean's training began at the Royal School of Needlework, London, in the early 1930s. Embroidery classes then concentrated almost entirely on the attainment of good technique. The Royal School was no exception. Its training was very thorough. Students were usually given designs to complete with little or no choice of fabrics or thread. Beryl Dean remembers being marked on the neatness of the back of her work, and being examined on the joining of threads for the most complicated of stitch techniques.

In 1932 Beryl Dean completed a piece titled *Madonna*, a portrait skilfully worked in Japanese gold thread. When the time came to apply for a job she was interviewed by F. W. Burroughs, then His Majesty's Inspector for Art. On seeing this piece he advised her to attend Grace Thompson's classes at the Bromley School of Art in order to take a more modern approach to design. Through Grace Thompson, Rebecca Crompton's influence was so strong that Beryl Dean felt she wanted to forget everything she had learnt! Subsequently she was awarded a Royal Exhibition to the Royal College of Art, London, and began a full-time career teaching many aspects of textile crafts including millinery and dressmaking.

Beryl Dean's work for contemporary ecclesiastical embroidery began when she questioned why embroidery for the Church remained so unaffected by design developments in other fields. When she found there were no examples to look to, she decided that it was up to her to bring about a change. From then on she focused her energy on introducing a modern approach to the design and carrying out of embroidery for the Church. Over forty years later she is the author of no less than seven books on the subject and has given lectures throughout Britain and the United States.

Her books contain chapters on symbolism, the practical aspects of making vestments and furnishings, commissions and group projects as well as on contemporary approaches to design. She also explains and demonstrates the practical application of gold and metal thread techniques traditionally found in the best ecclesiastical and secular embroidery of the past.

In May 1968 she was instrumental in organising an exhibition of contemporary ecclesiastical embroidery in the crypt of St Paul's Cathedral, London. The interest that this generated led to the formation of ecclesiastical embroidery groups all over Britain, and a revival in metal thread techniques generally. She has undertaken and involved many of her students in several superbly-executed commissions for cathedrals and churches in Britain. In 1975 she was awarded the MBE for her services to the Church.

I first saw her *Head of Christ* soon after it was completed. Although it was the smallest item in an exhibition of large-scale ecclesiastical works, its intensity claimed everyone's attention. Later in conversation about this piece, it emerged that she had embroidered it entirely for her own pleasure. While she was working on a very demanding commission, a longing to make the best possible use of her last remaining skeins of real Japanese gold thread grew very strong. Japanese gold is virtually unobtainable now. One afternoon, some two years on, the light from her sitting room window fell onto the polished surface of a table in such a way that, from her chair, in the grain of the wood she saw the face of Christ. The contours suggested a downward droop to his eyes. She knew she wanted to place all the emphasis on these eyes. The image was influenced by her love of Byzantine Art, but she knew it was also one which would lend itself readily to 'Or nué'. This is a technique she had learnt over sixty years ago at the Royal School. It is rarely practised now perhaps because it is not only one of the most difficult of techniques to perfect but also amongst the slowest to work. She describes it as the quintessence of all that is lovely in gold work.

Head of Christ Beryl Dean 1984
49·5cm × 45·5cm
including the wooden frame
Private collection (photo: Dudley Moss)

Photo detail 1

'**Or nué**' (shaded gold) is so called because the gold is shaded by the colour or pattern of the silk threads that fasten it down. The gold thread is couched down over the whole surface of the embroidery. Patterns and pictures emerge as the rows are covered with colour, or the gold glints between the carefully-spaced stitching (*photo detail 1*). Sometimes a positive image is left in the gold by stitching the background more densely, and vice versa (*photo detail 2*). Luminous, very subtle shading effects can be achieved through careful gradations of colour coupled with variable stitch spacings. The overall effect is of gold one way, and colour the other. The holding stitches can become a subtle decorative element in themselves. They can be worked over gold threads with great precision to form brick patterns, zig-zags, diaper and other decorative motifs.

As a form of needlepainting 'or nué' was perfected in the fifteenth and sixteenth centuries in Italy and Flanders. It provided the most effective means of interpreting the Baroque architecture and drapery featured in the paintings of the period. In those days very accurate coloured cartoons were prepared by artists and carried out by embroiderers in workshops under their supervision.

For this embroidery Beryl Dean traced a line drawing onto yellow linen prepared on a frame. Linen, because it helps to keep the lines straight, and yellow lest the background show between the rows of gold. The colours were selected from her stock of Filoselle silks. This is a pliant and soft thread which was produced in a wide range of graded colours but is now no longer available (*photo of materials*).

'Or nué' is exacting because each line has to be completed before the next is begun. Rather as in 'Fairisle' knitting, mistakes made a row or two back cannot be altered. Technically it is very difficult to keep the lines straight because solid areas of coloured stitching can crowd the spaces between the gold and cause bulges in the line. It is quite usual to have as many as fifty needles working at the same time. Artistically, it exercises the ability to use tonal values to create an image and to exploit all the possibilities given within the constraints of the technique (*photo detail 3*). Beryl Dean's love of good craftsmanship has remained with her. It is interesting that the motivation behind such an intense picture springs as much from a love of materials and technique as from the image it conveys. The fact that she has been able to fill a simple line drawing with colour over gold to express an image in her mind's eye, reflects her complete knowledge of the technique and a lifetime's experience.

Photo detail 2

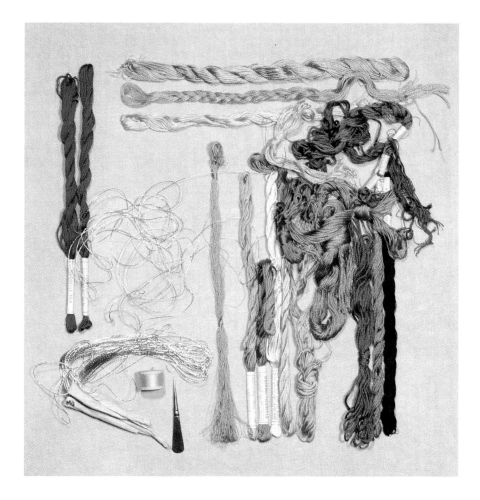

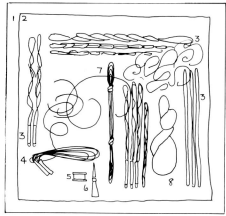

1, A frame covered with a backing fabric

2. Linen dyed yellow

3. Pearsall's Filoselle Silks

4. Real Japanese gold thread

5. Maltese silk for securing the gold

6. A stiletto or mellore

7. Horse tail silk, the perfect thread for couching gold

8. Silk darning threads, perfect for flesh tones

Photo detail 3

This detail of the panel extended by a stitch diagram illustrates how a simple line drawing is covered with couched gold.

If a piece of paper is placed on the embroidery and its straight edge moved horizontally up and down, the sequence of the stitching can be followed. This also reveals the subtle spacing and changes in colour along a single line of gold and the precise way in which the drawing is covered row by row. Notice how the drawing is modified by the structure of the technique.

The cut ends of a pair of gold threads are secured on the left-hand side and laid across the panel. Then a few couching stitches in thread to match the gold are worked before any colours are introduced. The couching stitches are always worked at right angles to the gold with a very fine needle and thread. When a stretch of colour is complete the needle still threaded is laid aside. Another needle is filled with the next colour and worked along the line, and so on. At the right-hand edge the two gold threads are secured and turned separately, one after the other, and then laid back across the panel. As the gold is taken from side to side up the panel it is very important to keep the rows straight and sufficiently apart without allowing gaps to appear. Included in the illustration of the materials used by Beryl Dean is her mellore, a special tool made for metal thread embroiderers. The spade end is used to smooth gold threads gently free of any crinkles, the pointed end to nudge them into place.

Index